Limited Liberty

The Legacy of Four Pentecostal Women Pioneers

Estrelda Y. Alexander

Seymour Press

Limited Liberty: The Legacy of Four Pentecostal Women Pioneers

Estrelda Y. Alexander

ISBN 13: 9781938373497
LCCN: 2020949461

Printed in the United States of America

Copyright 2020 Seymour Press
Capitol Heights, MD

CONTENTS

Preface

American women's lives changed dramatically in the forty years surrounding the turn of the twentieth century. Freed from many of the social constraints and expectations that previously consigned them to a life of housework and child-rearing, they took on increasingly visible roles in many public arenas, completing secondary school, matriculating from colleges, and entering the workforce in record numbers. With these achievements, they entered and excelled at occupations previously closed to them as attitudes about a woman's proper sphere began to be relaxed.

At the same time, the understanding of the roles that women were allowed to hold in the church was changing. With the ordination of Antoinette Brown by the Congregationalists in 1853, the door for pastoral and institutional leadership slowly began to inch open. In the next thirty years, 1853-1883, six denominations granted women ordination. From 1883 to 1923, thirteen others followed suit.[1] Even where ordination was granted, within mainline Protestantism it was generally expected that only a few "exceptional" women would pursue public ministry, and denominations rarely *welcomed* them wholeheartedly to the ranks of ordained clergy.

In the beginning, women in sectarian groups generally had a greater degree of freedom than their mainline sisters experienced. As the late-nineteenth-century Holiness movement birthed the early twentieth-century classical Pentecostal movement, women clergy played major roles. First with Charles Parham in his short-lived Topeka revival of 1901 and later with William Joseph Seymour in his long-running Azusa Street Revival, the movement evidenced an expanded view of women's proper place. Women were free to participate in and lead Pentecostal worship services. Women served as pastors, evangelists, or missionaries, carrying the Pentecostal gospel around the country and across the globe. They preached, taught, exhorted, and administered ordinances (sacraments) freely. They held governance positions in the loosely tied bodies and denominations that came into place in the new movement and were given a measure of autonomy in carrying out their ministries. But even here, the role of women was somewhat restricted. While they played larger roles than their sisters in mainline and evangelical denominations, women did not enjoy parity with their male colleagues. From the outset, they never attained what Mark Chavez has categorized as "full clergy rights"—the right to ordination to the highest rank of ministerial credentialing[2] within a denomination and, with it, the right to serve in positions of institutional leadership and governance at the highest levels.[3]

Several scholars have shown that, as the generally lower-class, sectarian movement attempted to gain respectability and take on characteristics of more middle-class evangelical denominations, the role of women ministers was increasingly curtailed.[4] Though women still preached and exhorted, leadership and governing roles were even more limited, as were opportunities to serve as pastors of viable congregations. Women who wanted to serve as pastors were often relegated to the task of church planting or nurturing new congregations. Further, once a congregation grew to the point of viability, a male colleague was often sent to take over the pastorate.

Pentecostal women who felt called to Christian service responded to the increasing restrictions on ministerial leadership in several ways. Some maintained a degree of autonomy and control by establishing or participating in primarily gender-restricted or gender-related groups such as women's auxiliaries, "willing workers," or pastor's aide societies. Others took on areas of less interest to men such as organizing mission societies or prayer bands. Some taught women's or children's Sunday school or Bible study classes. Some contented themselves with being perpetual church planters, assistant pastors, or traveling evangelists.

Still, others confined themselves to home responsibilities, giving up hope of having any meaningful clerical leadership role. These women continued to work within the limited nineteenth-century understanding of women's sphere. Although by the twentieth century that understanding was beginning to give way to a broader conception of women's place in society, it was least advanced within the conservative religious context in which they found themselves.

A few women, convinced that they had experienced an undeniable call of God to ministry and church leadership, refused to take a back seat. They acted on their Pentecostal beliefs that, like men, women were equally empowered by God through Holy Spirit baptism to undertake the ministry to which they were called. They did not seek permission from an existing body to preach or lead, but moved with deliberation to create environments in which they could be free to wholeheartedly pursue their calls.

Four Pentecostal pioneers—Mother Florence Louise Crawford (1871-1936), Bishop Mary Magdalena Lewis Tate (1871-1930), "Sister" Aimee Semple McPherson (1890-1944), and Bishop Ida Bell Robinson (1891-1944)—each decided to challenge ascribed roles for women within the Pentecostal movement by founding their own churches. Each used her unique gift for preaching and her charismatic personality to gather groups of faithful followers who eventually helped to grow scattered congregations into denominations with international constituencies.

Crawford established the Apostolic Faith Church[5] in 1907. Tate established the Church of the Living God, the Pillar and Ground of the Truth, Inc., in 1908. McPherson established the International Church of the Foursquare Gospel in 1924. Robinson founded the Mt. Sinai Holy Church of America, Inc., also in 1924. The distinctiveness of the names of their bodies highlights the specific contribution each woman saw herself making to the Pentecostal movement, for each felt that God had specifically ordained her to carry out the unique calling that name implied.

To varying degrees, the bodies they established have remained viable denominations. While having only a small U.S. presence, Crawford's body maintains an extensive international work. Tate's original group was the foundation for eight separate bodies, each of which traces its direct lineage back to this solitary woman. Robinson's group remained essentially intact, though it, in particular, has recently experienced substantial numerical decline, both in membership and in the number of congregations. McPherson's body is the one group that can be described as having flourished. It is the only one of the four that truly has a worldwide representation. The respective constituencies of these women range from little more than one hundred to several thousand congregations, representing several thousand to more than a million congregants. Two of these bodies, Tate's Church of the Living God and Robinson's Mt. Sinai Holy Church of America, Inc., have retained the leadership of women in the highest positions for a substantial portion of their history. All four

iv

groups continue to give women more freedom than is generally found in other contemporary Pentecostal denominations.

This work examines the lives, ministries, and theologies of these early-twentieth-century classical Pentecostal clergywomen with the intent of delineating the strategies they employed to secure leadership roles for themselves and other women clergy within the movement. The first task was to uncover historical resources relating to each woman's life, theology, and ministry. Where available, these resources include primary denominational sources (polities and doctrinal statements, periodicals, sermons, hymns, etc.), autobiographical works, and testimonials. More often, they are secondary sources, such as biographies of McPherson and biographical sketches of Tate and Robinson, souvenir journals from special denominational events (anniversaries, dedications, memorials, etc.), and several short articles.

The second task involves identifying each woman's distinctive accomplishments and contributions to women's leadership in the movement by developing a sociohistorical narrative of their lives, keeping four critical questions relating to strategies, social location, intention, and legacy in mind. What strategies did these women employ to build viable denominations where women's ministry and leadership could be freely exercised? What role did their respective cultural influences and social location play in the development of their respective denominations? To what extent did each woman develop and implement theologies and practices to encourage the continued leadership of women? Finally, to what extent did these women hold and act on a vision of systemic change in the situation of classical Pentecostal women?

The strategies that marginalized groups employ against a dominant group's unjust treatment generally fall into three categories-accommodation, reform, or activism.[6] This typology has characterized struggles for justice in various settings, including the African American civil rights movement, the Latin American liberation movement, and the modern feminist movement. It is specifically apropos for a critique of strategies women have employed in response to restricted church leadership within and outside of the Pentecostal movement.

Accommodationist strategies acknowledge the shared hopelessness of the injured parties of bringing material resolution to the unjust situation, while assisting them to make the best of it. Within the religious context, accommodationist strategies are generally employed by groups displaying other-worldly, revivalist expressions (such as found in Pentecostalism) that look for a reward or a reversal of injustice in the hereafter. Within Pentecostal women's struggle for full clergy rights, accommodationist strategies include accepting less than full ordination or lack of access to institutional leadership roles as God's will for women as revealed through an all-male hierarchy. Such a strategy is found among the women within a denomination or movement who—though sensing a personal call to public ministry—confine themselves to home responsibilities and give up hope of undertaking meaningful leadership roles.

Reform social injustice responses seek to integrate the injured group into the larger group in ways that are, at least minimally, acceptable to the larger group. They provide a limited critique of social arrangements within the given context without critically examining underlying relationships that foster injustice. They allow a means to protest the unjust structure in such a way that it remains unchanged. In reality, reform responses internalize the larger community's values to some degree and attempt to help the injured group incorporate these into their world view, making the group more acceptable. These strategies highlight social inequality, material success, individual achievement, and personal responsibility for failure and competition, but do not open up the larger group to the degree necessary to bring about equity.

Reform strategies for Pentecostal women's struggle for ministerial equity include filling lesser leadership roles—such as those of Sunday school teacher or evangelistic preacher-that keep them under the watchful control of male leaders and keep them from having access to top leadership roles such as those of head pastor or institutional administrator. Women who adopt these strategies see themselves as being "permitted" by male leadership to operate in certain roles in keeping with their submissive, complementarian position in the body of Christ.

Other reform strategies involve women contenting themselves with gender-segregated roles or areas of less interest to men, allowing themselves to maintain a degree of autonomy and control without threatening arenas in which men have a substantial stake. Further, within this context, if men's interest or stake is increased, women are subjected to the possibility of being supplanted and relegated to other areas limited to women's interest. Such was the case with early mission societies within mainline and evangelical circles, which men took over as their economic base increased.

Again, this pattern was representative of most traditional church planting efforts in early Pentecostalism. Repeatedly, women began new works, bringing them to viability, only to have a man take over pastoral leadership. The woman usually remained as an assistant or was sent to start another congregation to bring it to the same point. Denominational stances towards women's leadership did not change because of what these women accomplished. They were still viewed as less capable and suitable for leadership than their male colleagues.

Activist responses to social injustice change the injustice by questioning the system itself and/or demonstrating another way to be. They challenge the socio-historical and theological premises on which unjust actions are built and target the destruction of those foundations or elimination of their effect. The two types of activist responses-strategic and radical—differ mostly in degree. Both have the same goal: complete dismantling of the unjust system. Strategic activism identifies elements essential to the effective conduct of the unjust system and employs political, diplomatic, and systemic means to methodically eliminate their potential for causing injury or reduces the impact of that injury.

Strategic activism tactics include consciousness-raising; training leaders; providing financial, material, or spiritual support to causes and institutions; granting use of facilities for meetings; and developing separate institutions to meet the needs of the injured. Within the struggle for women's leadership in the church, strategic activist approaches would include the writing of feminist theologies and Bible study resources aimed at raising the consciousness of women and male church leaders.

On the other hand, radical activism employs extreme measures to bring dramatic changes to or overturn an unjust system and replace it with one that is just. These strategies challenge the unjust system itself, with the intent of bringing about systemic change that entirely eliminates or greatly reduces the effects of the injustice. Though seldom employed for women's struggle for parity within the Christian church, radical strategies might include staging demonstrations or sit-ins to disrupt the usual business of denominational meetings and call attention to women's plight, or agreeing, as a group, to withhold financial support such as tithes until certain conditions are met. They might also include forming coalitions to get women—or supportive male colleagues—elected to positions of leadership, or forming female religious movements that reject male leadership altogether. Radical activist strategies for addressing the issue of women's ministry and leadership have rarely, if ever, been employed within the context of classical Pentecostalism.

Modifying this typology provides a foundation for examining the strategies of the women we are interrogating. The paradigm, however, serves its greatest benefit if viewed as a continuum rather than a true typology. Elements of all three strategies are evident throughout these women's unfolding narratives, and neither could be categorized as purely accommodationist, reformist, or activist.

What was the role of cultural influences and social location in the development of their respective denominations? Clearly, none of us operates in a vacuum-in public or private life. Race, class, education, geography, and time in history impact who we are and what we do. Although all four women were products of working-class society, their lives, ministries, and theologies differ in important ways, fueled to some degree by their respective sociocultural locations. Crawford and McPherson were white, with all the privileges and entree that being white implied in early-twentieth-century North America-in the segregated Jim Crow period. Their geographical sphere was the fast, free, openness of the western frontier. Tate and Robinson were African American; they lived and worked in the rural south and urban end-points of the Great Migration. It is only fair to recognize the role these realities of their sociocultural location played in weighing and determining the impact of their individual lives and ministries. Further, one cannot gauge the import of their respective contributions without paying attention to these factors.

The third question is to what extent each woman developed and implemented theologies and practices to encourage the continued leadership of women. With their individual accomplishments, how did they assist, or fail to assist, other women in moving into leadership, and what did they do to ensure the continued leadership of women in their denominations beyond their lifetimes? Was this part of their calls, or did each simply count herself among the "few exceptional women" God sometimes—but rarely—calls?

The final question concerns the extent to which these women held and acted on a vision of systemic change in Pentecostal women's situation. Were they deliberately attempting to break open the wider Pentecostal movement to the increased, continued participation and leadership of women? Or were they simply content to pursue their personal ministry goals-with any advancement in the cause of women's leadership an inconsequential byproduct?

These issues and themes continually surface in their narratives. As we compare and evaluate their work, we see constructive and detrimental elements-some that should be emulated and some that might be discarded. The implications of the contributions of their individual and collective lives and ministries to women's religious history are twofold-the one socio-theological, the other practical.

Pentecostal women clergy find themselves having made some progress since the time of these early pioneers, a century ago. Yet, women's ordination to full clergy rights is still problematic in most larger Pentecostal denominations, and deployment patterns are still heavily gender-biased. Contemporary Pentecostal women struggle to gain full liberty within a tradition to which—though marginalized—they still hold allegiance. Hopefully, the model of these courageous foremothers will help sustain and embolden them.

INTRODUCTION

Women in Late-Nineteenth and Early-Twentieth-Century Religion

The almost seventy-five-year period encompassing the combined life spans of four extraordinary women—Florence Crawford, Mary Magdalena Lewis Tate, Aimee Semple McPherson, and Ida Robinson—witnessed substantial transformation in American women's lives. Dramatic changes occurred in society's view of what "woman's sphere" should encompass. Along with these came changes in women's status and broadening of arenas in which they were allowed to function. Although shifts began in the early nineteenth century, the rate of change accelerated greatly as the century ended.

Within the religious community, however, women's leadership was still severely restricted-though, even here, women began pushing more diligently for inclusion. Only four avenues of church leadership were generally open to women during this period: serving in the diaconate, foreign missions, missionary societies, and Christian education. Women entering diaconate ministry usually served as nurses or social workers in church-related or supported organizations. They engaged in church-sponsored humanitarian and benevolent efforts, including deaconess homes, modeled on the celibate Roman Catholic sisterhood, and introduced into the Protestant churches in the early 1900s. They also ventured into the seediest neighborhoods of the nation's bristling urban areas and founded settlement houses, clinics, and other social agencies principally to reach unchurched, down-and-out persons. Their constituents included alcoholics, prostitutes, and poor children and families whom the church had often not been able otherwise to reach.

Single women who sensed a call and/or sought vocational fulfillment within some phase of pastoral ministry likely found at least rudimentary fulfillment on the foreign mission field. But even here male denominational leaders were often reluctant to send them overseas, unless they agreed beforehand to live in a married household and confine themselves to roles that did not expose them to "undue danger or exertion." Other women, who felt "called" to public ministry and could accept a complementarian role,[2] could get some sense of fulfillment by marrying and working as "helpmates" to men who held leadership positions. As pastors' wives, deaconesses, or members of missionary households, these women often shouldered equal ministry responsibility with their husbands, though they were seldom given equal recognition.

Perhaps the greatest involvement of women in church leadership in the years surrounding the turn of the twentieth century was in establishing and supporting mission societies. Initially, these societies provided support without regard to gender. Further, they were more open to supporting women missionaries without the strings attached by male-dominated bodies. Women established separate structures to raise millions of dollars to support foreign and home missionaries. By the late 1920s, however, many of these organizations within established denominations had been merged with parallel, male-dominated organizations. In most cases, as a merger occurred, women's leadership was compromised, forcing the women to take secondary roles.

In Christian education, through the Sunday school movement, which had been established earlier in the nineteenth century, women were able to take on a number of responsibilities that men, in many cases, simply did not want. They organized citywide Sunday school societies and served as Sunday school teachers and superintendents. As in other areas, often once these ministries showed any sign of success, they were taken over by men.

Generally, women were excluded from mainline pulpits, though a few "exceptional women" had begun to move into a small number of pulpits in some denominations. In 1853, Congregationalist Antoinette

2

Brown became the first American woman to be ordained, though following her ordination she found little acceptance in Congregationalist pulpits. She was dismissed from her pastorate in 1854, eventually joining the Unitarian Church. Julia Foote became the first African American woman to gain ordination as a deacon in the African Methodist Episcopal Zion Church in 1894, only six years before her death. Her ordination came at the end of her extensive preaching career, for, though she had sought ordination earlier and was a renowned evangelist throughout most of her life, she was denied it until then.

Several mainline denominations changed their polity to grant women limited ordination. Many allowed women the right to preach but denied them access to institutional leadership roles. Others granted women access to ecclesial leadership, but denied them the right to preach. However, in the new sectarian movements, including the Shakers and Christian Scientists, women found openness to religious leadership. These groups maintained a place of prominence for women's leadership past their initial stages and included recognition of the right of women to serve in leadership as part of their ongoing ethos. Largely because of these groups' egalitarian stances, women were attracted to them in large numbers.

Two religious movements—the Holiness movement that came into maturity during the end of the nineteenth century and the Pentecostal movement birthed at the beginning of the twentieth—held promise of greater participation in ministry and leadership for women (and other marginalized groups), attracting these groups in large numbers. However, while women continued to find widespread acceptance as leaders throughout most of the history of the Holiness movement, this has been less true for the story of women's role within Pentecostalism.

Following the sect-type pattern identified by Max Weber, women played major roles in the early stages of the Pentecostal movement. According to Weber, as new religious movements are in the formative, sect stage, they depend for leadership on charismatic rather than hierarchical structures. These groups, therefore, allow room for women and other persons who would otherwise be overlooked for leadership roles. As these groups grow into more formalized, denominational structures, charismatic leadership is "routinized" into more traditional patterns that marginalize women's leadership.[3]

Before World War I, while many sociologists of religion still classified the Pentecostal movement as a sect, women were given "limited" freedom to pastor churches, serve as missionaries, preach, teach, exhort, and carry out other areas of ministry as was needed and as they desired. With some restrictions, they had autonomy in carrying out their ministries as they saw fit and had a role in governance and leadership. In all, the leadership role of women in these movements was generally greater than that of their sisters in other Evangelical or mainline denominations.

As time passed and the movement attempted to gain more respectability and take on more of the characteristics of middle-class denominations—whether mainline or Evangelical—the role of women was curtailed. Though women still had the freedom to preach and exhort, leadership and governing roles became more limited, and women's ministry and leadership looked more like the hierarchy they once denounced in mainline bodies.

Caught in this changing situation, between pre- and post- World War I Pentecostalism, women responded in several ways. Some established or involved themselves in gender-related groups such as women's auxiliaries and pastor's aid societies, to maintain some degree of autonomy and control over the areas of religious life pertaining primarily to women. Others took on areas of less interest to men, such

4

as organizing missionary societies or prayer bands to support the spiritual needs of the church. Still, others, who bought into conservative arguments of women's sphere and views of a woman's place, confined themselves to home responsibilities and gave up hope of undertaking meaningful leadership roles in the church.

There were, however, a few daring women who refused to take a back seat in ministry and leadership. Instead, as early practical biblical feminists (though they would not assume that label) they challenged—on what they believed to be biblical grounds—unjust restrictions on the scope of their ministries and the role of women in the church and society. Their warrant for the challenge they mounted was an understanding of the prophetic witness of the Joel 2:28 passage as including both sons and daughters, servants, and handmaidens on whom the Spirit would be poured. With this understanding, they were willing to stand against any restriction the church sought to impose and instead to do exactly what they felt called of God to do.

Some of these women found male colleagues with whom they could work as equals in building up newly established organizations. For example, Catherine Booth, the wife of William Booth and an excellent preacher in her own right, is acknowledged by historians as playing a prominent role in the founding and leadership of the Salvation Army, a Holiness body. Her daughter, Evangeline, was also an excellent preacher who was later prominent in the leadership of the Salvation Army. Another holiness pioneer, Mary Lee Cadle, founded eighteen congregations that later merged with the body that became the Church of the Nazarene in 1908.

The four women pioneers in this study—Crawford, Tate, McPherson, and Robinson—had a different response to the lack of freedom they found. Each openly challenged the restrictions within the early Pentecostal movement. They chose to found independent congregations rather than be limited by the respective situations of the bodies in which they were involved. In each case, these congregations became denominations that grew over time to encompass international as well as American constituencies.

Each woman can be squarely placed within the Pentecostal tradition, for each held to the major tenets of Pentecostalism. Yet, each added to the tradition her unique understanding of Pentecostal spirituality and distinctive elements that carried the indelible stamp of her personality. Among these was an unswerving affirmation of her right as a woman to operate in the full freedom of the Spirit in whatever capacity of church leadership she felt called.

Women in the Early Pentecostal Movement

The beginning of the twentieth-century Pentecostal movement is variously placed at either New Year's Day 1901 in Topeka, Kansas, under the leadership of Charles Fox Parham or April 1906 in Los Angeles, California, under the leadership of William Joseph Seymour. A more critical view sees these two dates as integrally related as part of the infancy of an ongoing, dynamic religious movement that continues to grow and evolve. Together, they form the joint historical base that has an even deeper foundation in the nineteenth-century Wesleyan Holiness movement and is tied to the present-day Charismatic Renewal movement.

The Pentecostal movement appropriated the Holiness understanding that the baptism of the Holy Spirit is a separate work of grace that follows upon salvation within the believer's life and is an essential part of normal Christian experience. Pentecostalism added to this understanding the doctrine that a specific outward sign—speaking in tongues (glossolalia)—is the initial evidence of Holy Spirit baptism. To Pentecostals, this "outpouring" or "infilling" of the Spirit endows the believer with supernatural empowerment both to live a "holy" life and to accomplish "works of righteousness" for the Kingdom of God.

Its adherents seek to establish personal communion with God through ecstatic religious experience—specifically glossolalia—as evidence that such an outpouring and infilling has taken place.

Those who see Parham, the former Methodist Episcopal preacher who embraced the nineteenth-century Holiness revival, as the leader of the movement claim the 1901 beginning. He is generally given credit for crafting and widely disseminating the doctrine that glossolalia is the initial evidence of one's having received the baptism of the Holy Spirit, and with igniting the spark that set Pentecostalism on its path as the most prolific religious movement since the Reformation.[5]

In 1900, Parham established the Bethel Bible School and Healing Home in Topeka, Kansas. His primary reason for doing so was to promulgate his understanding of Holy Spirit baptism, along with several other restorationist views. The other reason he did so was to practice his faith healing ministry. By December of that year, Parham had led his forty students through a study of the major tenets of the Holiness movement, including sanctification, the baptism of the Holy Spirit, and divine healing. As part of their study, they were asked to search the Bible for evidence of what generally accompanied the reception of the baptism of the Holy Spirit. After a period of study, they unanimously confirmed Parham's belief that glossolalia-speaking in tongues-was that evidence.

Parham continued to conduct revival meetings throughout the early part of 1901. During this time, he claimed that several of his students spoke in at least one of twenty-one distinctive languages, including French, German, Swedish, Chinese, Japanese, Hungarian, Bulgarian, Russian, and Italian.[6] At some point, Parham himself had the experience of speaking in tongues. Through this series of meetings, he gained several adherents to his doctrine. However, the revivals never proved to be big successes and largely went unnoticed by other Holiness leaders.

These episodes of glossolalia with Parham and his followers, were not, in themselves, unique. Several movements throughout history had evidenced episodes of ecstatic religious experience involving glossolalia. Tongues have played a part in every modern revival movement since the Reformation, including the Great Awakening and the nineteenth-century Holiness movement. What was distinctive about what occurred at Parham's Topeka Bible school and the subsequent Azusa Street meetings was that, for the first time, the concept of being baptized with the Holy Spirit was specifically linked to the outward sign of speaking in tongues. Further, this was the first time the experience was confirmed as legitimate and adopted as a practice by members of several loosely related Christian traditions. Most of mainline Christianity, however, still considered the phenomenon heretical, saw it as some type of oddity, or ignored it altogether.

In 1905, Parham reestablished his headquarters in Houston, Texas, established another Bible school, and began training ministers in his distinctive doctrine of divine healing and tongues as initial evidence. However, Parham's leadership never matured into anything more than that of a Bible school instructor and traveling evangelist. The prolonged, widespread Pentecostal revival for which he had hoped and worked never materialized under him. Rather, it was at his Bible school that leadership for the fledgling Pentecostal movement arose from an unsuspected arena. As social analyst, Robert Anderson, characterizes the shift in leadership: "[w]hat had been under Parham a relatively small, localized movement, was to assume international proportions through the Los Angeles ministry of an obscure, chunky [sic], black man."[7]

In spring 1906, William Seymour, a largely self-educated son of former slaves, found himself a student at Parham's school. Because of rigid segregation laws, Seymour was forced to place himself just outside

8

the door to listen in as white students were instructed. He stayed in this uncomfortable situation only long enough to get the meat of Parham's teaching. By the time he left, he was poised to become the catalytic agent for a fresh revival movement that within only a few years would eclipse that of his former teacher and spread throughout the United States and many other countries of the world.

By April, Seymour was in Los Angeles at the invitation of an African American Holiness congregation, to presumably serve as its associate pastor. Though this invitation resulted in a disagreement over the initial evidence doctrine, Seymour began a home Bible study, and, shortly before Easter, seven of the faithful experienced speaking in tongues. As news of the incident spread through the community, attendance grew and the meeting moved from the front room to the porch of the home. People gathered there and in the street for several days to hear his teaching. The group then found and rented a converted livery stable at 312 Azusa Street from the African Methodist Episcopal Church to continue their still growing meetings.

Camp meeting style worship services were held daily, generally lasting for several hours and running from ten in the morning until midnight. These ecstatic services included, along with speaking in tongues, impromptu sermons, prophesying, singing in tongues, interpretation of tongues, conversions, divine healing, and exorcisms. Within several days of the start of the revival, the local media, including the Los Angeles Times, began to take notice of what was happening in this little regarded section of town, among a little regarded group of people. They sent reporters, who captured the essence of what they observed and critically, and often sarcastically, reported it to the city and the rest of the world. What they reported was "a weird babel of tongues" among people who "practice the most fanatical rites, preach the weirdest theories, and work themselves into a state of trance in their peculiar zeal."[8]

These stories, along with those in *The Apostolic Faith*, word of mouth communications, letters, and correspondences attendees sent to loved ones and acquaintances, formed the nucleus of information about the revival. They drew a steady crowd of seekers almost from the beginning. Some were simply curious; some were skeptics who came to convince Seymour and his followers to abandon their fanatical antics and heretical beliefs. Some were seeking a closer relationship with God and wanted to add another religious experience to their lives.

Another prominent feature of these meetings was their radically egalitarian nature. People of different races came together in an unprecedented manner to experience this "new religion." Blacks, whites, Hispanics, and Asians worshiped side by side. The degree of racial harmony of the meetings led one prominent participant to report in his memoirs that "the color line was washed away in the blood [of Jesus]."[9] Another characterization put it more explicitly:

> It was something very extraordinary, that white pastors from the South were eagerly prepared to go to Los Angeles to Negroes [sic], to fellowship with them and to receive through their prayers and intercessions the blessings of the Spirit. And it was still more wonderful that these white pastors went back to the South and reported that they had been together with Negroes [sic], that they had prayed in one Spirit and received the same blessing as they.[10]

Though most worshipers were from lower and working classes, there was no stratification by class, race, gender, or age in participation or leadership in the services. Women, as well as men, enjoyed the freedom to minister within the services as they felt God leading them. Even children who felt inspired by God had a voice in the worship. Ecclesiastical credentials or education played little part in determining a person's role in the meetings. Rather, people felt directed by the Holy Spirit to testify, sing, exhort, pray, or preach with the blessing of Seymour and others of those in "leadership."

Seymour's acceptance of Parham's teaching on divine healing played a prominent part in these meetings as people prayed for the sick and reported miraculous reversals in their sickly physical condition. Other gifts of the spirit were in evidence as men and women prophesied, gave words of wisdom or knowledge, exhorted, and interpreted messages previously spoken in tongues as prompted by the Spirit.

The understanding of ministry throughout early Pentecostalism closely followed the Azusa Street pattern and was largely a lay matter based on a sectarian understanding of what constituted a call. It relied on personal testimony or affirmation of such a call rather than an ecclesial endorsement. Acceptance of that testimony by a congregation revolved around perceived Holy Spirit empowerment, a sense of God-ordained destiny, and endowment with specific spiritual gifts to make ministry effective. Early Pentecostals felt that the Holy Spirit, rather than church hierarchy, was the arbiter of a person's fitness for ministry.

Within this context, most of the earliest Pentecostals deemed ministerial credentialing as relatively unimportant. Some saw themselves as simply "ordained by the Lord" and needing no human agency to affirm their ministerial status. For them, the fruit of their accomplishments demonstrated whether they were truly called. Others were informally set apart for ministry by the laying on of hands in a home meeting or other nontraditional setting. Some held credentials from local mission churches, but for them the most important function formal credentialing served was to permit them to obtain cut-rate ministerial railroad fare, allowing them to get from one preaching engagement to another affordably.

The Azusa Street revival lasted eight years. By its end, in 1914, there were more than twenty denominations and several hundred congregations in the United States that identified themselves as Pentecostal and holding to the doctrine of initial evidence. In the twenty years following the close of the revival, several more denominations and several thousand congregations in the United States were established and several hundred more existing congregations had switched to the Pentecostal camp. By that time, the Pentecostal message had been heard all over the world. Women, as well as men, communicated that message and helped establish and build up these congregations and denominations.

Women in Ministry

Charles Parham organized his Bible school in Topeka Kansas to "fit men and women to go to the ends of the earth to preach."[11] He ordained women as well as men and commissioned them to ministry. Many of these women and men assisted Parham in his evangelistic campaigns that he conducted throughout the country. It was a woman under Parham's leadership who is credited by many with ushering in the entire modern Pentecostal movement.

On New Year's Eve, December 31, 1900, three months after establishing the school, Parham conducted a watch night service for several students and sympathizers. During the service, a female student, Agnes Ozman, requested him to lay hands on her to receive the baptism of the Holy Spirit. Shortly after midnight on January 1, 1901, after several requests from Ozman, an at-first reluctant Parham agreed. As he anointed her with oil, laid hands on her, and prayed, she reportedly began speaking in a fluent Chinese tongue and was unable to speak in English for three days following this experience. Additionally, it is reported that when she attempted to write during those three days, she wrote in Chinese characters.[12]

Her name, therefore, and not Parham's or Seymour's, is immortalized as the first to publicly speak in tongues in twentieth-century America as the initial evidence of Holy Spirit baptism. After her Pentecostal experience, Ozman started almost immediately to evangelize throughout the Midwest. She later married Philemon LaBerge and joined with him in conducting revival meetings and camp meetings primarily in the Midwest. For a period, around 1911, she was affiliated with the Pentecostal Holiness Church and served that denomination in Oklahoma City, Oklahoma. In 1917, she affiliated with the Assemblies of God, receiving credentials as an evangelist.[13]

As in Parham's ministry, women played a prominent role in the Azusa Street Revival and the Apostolic Faith Mission that grew out of it. It was a woman who introduced Seymour to the distinctively Pentecostal doctrine of tongues as initial evidence of baptism of the Holy Spirit. A woman was the catalyst for the move of Seymour's ministry to Los Angeles. Women were prominently evident in every aspect of the leadership of the revival and the local church that grew out of it. Women were important in moving the Pentecostal message from Azusa Street across the United States and around the world. Indeed, an overview of women's involvement with the revival leads one to conclude that the impact of what occurred at the Azusa Street meeting would have been greatly reduced had women not been involved. Since Parham tended to operate on a somewhat more hierarchical and individualistic model, it is worth questioning whether his ministry might have enjoyed more success if he had given women a more prominent place.

Lucy Farrow introduced Seymour to the doctrine and experience of the Holy Spirit baptism with tongues. Farrow had been a governess for Parham's family and had been allowed to listen to his lectures on the baptism of the Holy Spirit at his Healing Home and Bible School. While in Houston, where she was active in the Holiness movement,

13

Seymour heard her speak in tongues in a worship service. When he asked Farrow about her experience, she explained what she had learned from Parham about the doctrine of initial evidence and then introduced Seymour to Parham. She followed Seymour to Los Angeles to assist in teaching at the Bonnie Brae Bible study and to work beside him at Azusa Street. After leaving there, she established a church in Norfolk, Virginia, then traveled as a missionary to Africa.

Of the twelve elders originally appointed to handle the finances, correspondences, and examination of persons for ordination at the Azusa Street Mission, six were female. Five of these six-Lucy Farrow, Ophelia Wiley, Mrs. G. W. Evans, Clara Lum, and Florence Crawford-were to play important roles in the upstart movement. Little is known of the extent of involvement of the other woman, Phoebe Sargent, in the mission or of what other ministries she was involved in outside the mission. Crawford's ten-year-old daughter also participated in the mission.

Some credit Crawford as being the first of its converts to take the Pentecostal message on the revival circuit. Crawford was instrumental in distributing the more or less monthly newspaper, *The Apostolic Faith*, which chronicled the revival's events to its supporters. Eventually, she and Seymour disagreed regarding his decision to marry, and Crawford took the newsletter mailing list to Portland.

Clara Lum served as secretary of the mission, a member of its governing board, and co-editor (with Seymour) of *The Apostolic Faith* from 1906 to 1908. She, like Crawford, objected to Seymour's marriage to Jennie Moore, left the mission, and moved to Oregon, corroborating with Crawford in taking the national and international mailing, and leaving Seymour with only the Los Angeles list. She later joined with Crawford and the two began republishing the newsletter, at first without acknowledging that Seymour was no longer affiliated with it.[14]

Though not initially an elder at the Azusa Street Mission, Jennie Moore was present at the Bonnie Brae prayer meetings. Moore was one of Seymour's earliest adherents to experience the baptism of the Holy Spirit with tongues and reportedly "played the piano in the Spirit" without prior training.[15] She went with Seymour to Azusa Street and was an active participant in the revival and the leadership of the church. She and Seymour later married and, during his lifetime, she worked alongside him in leading the mission. Upon his death, she served as pastor of the then dwindling mission.

Several outstanding women were among the many evangelists and missionaries who went out from the Azusa Street revival to take the message of Pentecostalism across the country and around the world.[16] Ophelia Wiley preached from time to time in the Azusa Street meetings and authored articles for *The Apostolic Faith*. She also went out as part of evangelistic teams to spread the news of the revival in various cities throughout the northwestern United States. Ivey Campbell preached revivals throughout Ohio and Pennsylvania and won many to the Pentecostal experience. Louisa Condit went first to Oakland, California, and then to Jerusalem. Lucy Leatherman traveled around the world conducting evangelistic meetings. She first went to Oakland, California, then to Colorado Springs and Denver, Colorado, and New York before embarking as a missionary to Israel, Egypt, Palestine, and later to Chile and Argentina. By the time she visited Argentina, she had joined with the Church of God and is credited with helping to establish the denomination in that country. She reportedly received the gifts of xenolalia and was able to speak Arabic.

Julia Hutchins took the Pentecostal message to Africa. Hutchins had been the pastor whose church originally objected to Seymour's identification of tongues with the baptism of the Holy Spirit and locked him out. She was later won to his point of view and, after affiliating with Seymour's mission for a while, she traveled as a missionary, preaching in several U.S. cities before taking the Pentecostal message to Liberia.

Often missionary couples were sent out from Azusa Street both as revivalists and missionaries. The women in these couples not only accompanied their husbands to play the expected role of a supportive minister's wife. They were also actively involved in every aspect of ministry: preaching, teaching, and praying for the sick and converts. Among those who moved out from Azusa Street were Abundio and Rosa Lopez. They worked the altars at the Azusa Street meetings and held street services in Los Angeles' Hispanic sections. G. W. and Daisy Batman went as missionaries to Liberia. Samuel and Ardell Mead had been holiness missionaries to Liberia for twenty years before the start of the revival. After testifying to having had the Pentecostal experience of Holy Spirit baptism, they returned to the mission field and helped spread the Pentecostal message.

Some observers have characterized Pentecostalism as essentially "women's religion" because of the greater proportion of women than men who have historically participated in the movement.[17] However, women's experience within Pentecostalism has been mixed. From the beginning, they were attracted to the movement in larger numbers than men and took on roles from bench members and worshipers to Bible teachers, evangelists, and pastors. Women ministers within early Pentecostalism enjoyed a greater degree of freedom than their contemporaries in most other branches of the Christian church— except their Holiness forerunners.

On close examination, examples of women's leadership abound from the beginning of the movement. In those earliest years, there appeared to be almost absolute freedom for women to pursue whatever course they felt God was leading them to follow. According to one historian, "Women were so prominent in early Pentecostalism... that even some Pentecostals lamented ' the effeminacy of our present ministry."[18] Due in part, however, to attitudes such as this, this apparent freed rein lasted only a few years and quickly gave way to several formal and informal restrictions on the roles women could play within most Pentecostal bodies.

Upon closer examination, women's freedom was more perceived than real and varied widely among various factions of the movement. Several Pentecostal denominations granted women what Mark Chavez defines as "full clergy rights—ordination, and all the rights and privileges inherent with it—from their inception. According to Chavez, denominations that grant full clergy rights are those in which there is "formally unrestricted access [for women] to all religious positions within a denomination." He distinguishes that from denominations that grant women ordination or license them for ministry but bar them from holding institutional leadership.[19]

The Pentecostal Holiness Church, which began as a Holiness body in 1895 and later adopted Pentecostal doctrinal statements into its polity, was among the first Pentecostal bodies to grant women full clergy rights.[20] As late as 1935, the Open Bible Standard Churches, one of the bodies to be founded as an offshoot of McPherson's International Church of the Foursquare Gospel, also incorporated full ordination for women as part of its founding polity.[21] Many other Pentecostal denominations granted women "limited ordination" or credentialing without governing authority. For example, in the United Holy Church, out of which Ida Robinson came, women were licensed or ordained to ministry but received little material or spiritual support from male colleagues, who only tolerated them.

Even where the official dogma concerning women clergy was egalitarian, the unofficial tradition concerning "male-only" leadership was often not noticeably different from other traditions. While official doctrine or polity made all levels of ministry open to all called and qualified men and women, this unofficial stance still held that only men

17

could hope to hold the top positions, such as presiding elder, district overseer or superintendent, bishop, or other denominational head; and women could not hope to be appointed as pastor of viable congregations.

As Pentecostal historian, Edith Blumhofer, succinctly characterizes the situation:

> [P]entecostals have always had reservations about women who departed from their "proper sphere." Like their other evangelical contemporaries, [P]entecostals authenticated the witness of "prophesying daughters." They also usually denied women any institutional presence. Pentecostal women flourished as evangelists and missionaries, but not as pastors or denominational leaders. They enjoyed cultural authority but not institutional voice.[22]

The original freedom given to women in the Pentecostal movement, even when it was limited-resulted from several factors. First, Pentecostal eschatology supported the premillennial understanding popular in the period in which the movement began. Early Pentecostals saw their revival as a fulfillment of the biblical prophecy of Joel 2:28. Within this understanding, the Pentecost scenario in Acts chapter 2 constituted the "former rain" and the Azusa Street revival constituted the "latter rain"—the culmination of the "age of the Spirit." Early Pentecostals saw themselves as living in the last days, before the return of Christ, when He would establish His millennial realm of peace on earth. With this understanding, they also held the belief that anyone who was not a born-again Christian (was not "saved") at Christ's return would be doomed to eternal hell. They felt an urgent need to enlist everyone in the business of winning as many souls into God's realm as possible before the end of time.

18

Therefore, women as well as men were enlisted to preach the gospel and win souls in whatever venue they found themselves.

Second, there was an understanding that individuals were empowered through Holy Spirit baptism to do ministry as the Spirit willed. They saw themselves as living in a time when God would supernaturally anoint both men and women, without regard to social constrictions, education, or other formal preparation, to accomplish this task. The proof of whether or not one was called to the ministry lay in the person's testimony to such a call and the perceived fruit of a Spirit-empowered ministry, rather than in any formal ecclesiastical system of selection or promotion. Those who demonstrated preaching skill and the ability to convey a convincing gospel message, and who displayed charismatic ministry gifts such as divine healing and exorcisms and the ability to win others to salvation were enlisted into action. It did not matter whether they were women or men. This understanding of ministry was coupled with a general disdain for hierarchical church structures and denominationalism, at least at first. Such disdain resulted in a radical egalitarianism in the early period of the movement and, therefore, greater opportunity for women than in many other denominations.[23]

Summarizing the effects of the egalitarian understanding fostered in the ministry of women in the Pentecostal movement, an editor of an early Pentecostal periodical wrote: "Obscure men and women, boys and girls, have received from God definite calls of this 'latter-day' outpouring is the Apostolate of women They did not push themselves to the front, God pulled them. They did not take this ministry on themselves, God put it on them."[24] Yet competing theologies complicated the status and freedom of women ministers in the early movement. Preaching women modeled themselves after their Holiness predecessors, who also took their authority from the Joel 2:28 passage, "your sons and daughters shall prophesy," and held to a radical concept

19

of the equality of the sexes in ministry. However, restorationist elements within Pentecostalism sought to return the church to "New Testament simplicity and purity." For some, an essential rudiment of this restoration was the felt need to follow Pauline restrictions on the ministry of women within the church.

Pentecostals also sought to distance themselves from association with modernity and "worldliness," including any ideas of the "new woman" that were coming into fashion as the movement emerged. They sought by outward appearance and social constraints, and rhetoric, to ensure that there was a recognizable distinction between the modern, "unsaved" world and themselves. They saw the women's movement as threatening the God-ordained social order prescribed in scripture and representing rebellion against God.

From the movement's inception, Pentecostal women, as well as men, tended to hold the conservative understanding of women's role within the family and society that only deepened when the movement sought to align itself more closely with the broader Evangelical community. Like other segments of that community and broader society, early Pentecostals believed that the proper place for women was in the home. Married women were expected to uphold the role of submission to their husbands and were generally expected to be supportive of their husband's work and/or ministry. Nonetheless, like other evangelicals, it made a place for those few exceptional women whom God might choose to use in an extraordinary way.

In some denominations, a specific but often unofficial limitation faced by women was pastoral placement. Leaders generally gave women the freedom to "dig out," or plant, congregations and nurture them to the point of viability. They were also encouraged to take on congregations that were at the point of failure and use their preaching, evangelism, and administration gifts to rebuild them to viability. Once these congregations grew to sizeable membership that could economically sustain the salary of a full-time pastor-as well as other financial obligations of the local church—denominational leaders would replace the woman with a new, male pastor. Leaders then sent the woman to another community to dig out another new work or repair another failing congregation. Over several decades, a woman might start or renew several congregations in this manner but would never be allowed to take any of them past this point.[25]

Leaders also sent male ministers to plant new churches or bring failing congregations back to a point of viability. They often replaced these men with a new pastor once the planter brought a congregation to a viable point. For men who were successful in this endeavor, however, replacement often meant promotion to a larger congregation-rather than starting all over in similarly dire circumstances. The thinking of leaders in limiting women in this way was undergirded by two major rationales. First, some Pentecostal denominations prohibited women from carrying out the ordinances of the church and from conducting the business of the local congregation. These leaders felt that women would not regularly have to do either so long as the congregations were small and struggling. When the occasion arose for carrying out ordinances or conducting meetings, leaders expected and encouraged women to call a male colleague from a neighboring congregation within the denomination.[26]

Second, many leaders felt that women could depend on the incomes of their husbands or some other male relative to provide for their material needs. Therefore, they felt that women did not require the same level of financial support as their male colleagues. Since this was believed to be the case, when a congregation became financially viable, these leaders felt it necessary to give the leadership of the congregation to a male minister who would have to depend on the finances to support his family. They would then send the woman to a new, or smaller, congregation that could not provide adequate support for a full-time pastor. Women who wished to remain in ministry within existing denominations were faced with accepting these limitations. Those who felt called to pastoral ministry accepted the inequitable life of a perpetual church planter. Other women took to the evangelistic circuit, preaching wherever they were asked and accepting whatever "love offering" a congregation was willing or could afford to give them.

Early Pentecostal Denominations

Specific examples of the stance of loosely organized Pentecostal bodies and more structured denominations illustrate the mixed situation for women in the early Pentecostal movement. The involvement of women in ministry in three early classical Pentecostal denominations—the Church of God in Christ, the Assemblies of God, and the Church of God (Cleveland, Tenn.)-demonstrate how the apparent freedom in ministry quickly gave way to limited freedom, then to gradually increasing, formal restrictions on the ministry and leadership of women.

The Church of God in Christ

The Church of God in Christ (COGIC) came into being within a year of the start of the Azusa Street Revival. Charles Harrison Mason, its African American founder, came to Azusa Street partially on the prodding of his co-laborer, Charles Price Jones. Once there, Mason accepted the Pentecostal message. When he returned to tell Jones and their constituents about his new understanding, Jones rejected the doctrine and experience and the two eventually severed ties. The remnant that remained with Jones founded the Church of Christ (Holiness). Mason's group ultimately retained the name, Church of God in Christ, and became a Pentecostal body.[27]

Within that body—which with eight million members is arguably the largest Pentecostal denomination in the United States and definitely the largest African American Pentecostal body in the country—the ministry of women was restricted from the outset. Drawing on his Baptist roots, Mason, saw women playing a "vital" but distinctive role from men. Within this role, Mason "restricted [women's] influence by preserving the office of pastor and title of preacher for men. Women expounding on scripture were said to be teaching—not preaching—and were allowed to speak only from a secondary lectern, not from the pulpit."[28]

Ithiel Clemmons, late COGIC historian and Mason biographer justified the founder's stance this way:

> By forming a unique church structure [for women]... the denomination harnessed the spiritual fervor, mental acumen, physical energy, and economic potential of its female members while maintaining male authority. As a result, the church cultivated female leadership without alienating the men, took advantage of women's abilities to "plant" new congregations without authorizing them to preach or pastor, and established an auxiliary structure that sustained basic [P]entecostal-Holiness church doctrine through periods of strife among the church's male leaders [29]

As Clemmons euphemistically interpreted these limitations, COGIC women "function[ed] in the ambivalent position of shared, but secondary authority... preserv[ing] the male dominance that conformed the denomination to biblical imperatives"[30] Within this formally instituted structure, women could not be ordained to pastoral ministry, but could be licensed as "evangelists" or "missionaries"[31] to preach and teach primarily other women and work in what the COGIC leadership termed "vital" roles. In these roles, women could raise funds for local congregations and the national denomination; direct local,

23

regional, and national women's programs; and provide material support for the pastor and his family. During the ninety-five-year history of the denomination, this dual structure has remained in place and the real restrictions on the ministry of women have continued.

The Assemblies of God

When the first General Council of the Assemblies of God met in 1914, in Hot Springs, Arkansas, to organize itself into a body, almost one-third of the delegates were women ministers. Though such a large number of women were present, the body authorized the ordination of women only as evangelists and missionaries, explicitly denying them the right to serve in pastoral ministry or any position involving holding authority over men.[32] Later that year, women missionaries serving outside the United States were granted the right to perform funerals, marriages, baptisms, and communion, in case of an emergency and when a man was not available.[33]

In 1917, the General Council dropped distinctions of ordination as evangelist, missionary, and elder (pastor) and voted that all ordination be "to the full gospel ministry." However, the council did not lift the practical restrictions on women's ministry so that (except for missionaries) they still were unable to perform the ordinances (or sacraments).[34] In 1919, that same body restricted the vote to male ministers only,[35] but in 1920, the Council had an apparent change of heart and granted women the right to vote.[36] Women clergy[37] in the United States were not given the right to perform the sacraments on an emergency basis until 1922.[38] Further, it was not until 1935 that women were granted full ordination-full clergy rights-without restriction on serving or voting.[39] Even this concession did not, however, materially improve the ministry of most women or reduce the predominance of male leadership at congregational and administrative levels.

24

Church of God (Cleveland, Tennessee)

Early Church of God sources contend that "five of the seven founding fathers of the Church of God (Cleveland, Tenn.) were, actually, founding mothers. This characterization highlights the fact that at the 1898 meeting that saw the creation of the Christian Union (that eventually became the Church of God), the majority of persons who initially stepped forward when Richard Spurling gave the invitation to form the organization were women, and women have played an important but decreasing role in the denomination since its beginning. Initially, they were encouraged to serve as evangelists and pastors and to preach and teach wherever they could. However, again, the leadership of women incurred some limitation from the outset. The story of the Church of God is an example of how such limitations quickly grew and spread.

By the end of its second General Assembly in 1907, reports from Church of God congregations indicated that the group had substantially more women adherents than men.[41] Although women were frequent speakers and had full voting rights in the early General Assemblies, increasingly more restrictive measures were put in place with every succeeding session. Within a few years, the rights of women to serve in leadership roles within the body were almost entirely reduced to a few highly prescribed functions.

The third General Assembly in 1908 declared that "women who are qualified and feel the call to work should be appointed by the churches" (as pastors).[42] These women were given the title of deacon and, apparently, had the same rights and privileges as their male counterparts. One year later, the fourth General Assembly determined that women should not be ordained because there was a "lack of precept and example in the New Testament" for such ordination. Further, it was determined that, at least for the short term, wives of

25

deacons would be considered deaconesses "by virtue of the position and ordination of their husbands."[43] With this move, a woman-no matter how her gifted or called—could not become a deaconess unless married to a deacon. In 1912, the Assembly decided that women should have no part in business meetings of the sessions.[44] The 1913 Assembly precluded women ministers from performing marriages and taking part in the business and government of local congregations.[45] During the 1916 meeting, the Body of Elders, made up of ordained ministers, was formed. It had responsibility for conducting the business of the denomination through the General Assembly. Since only ordained ministers could be a part of this body and vote, this solidified the 1913 motion concerning women not being involved in the business of the denomination, as well as taking the vote away from laymen.[46]

By 1926, the General Assembly decided that there should be different licenses for male and female evangelists. The male license specifically granted men the authority to "establish churches, baptize converts, administer the Lord's Supper, and the washing of saints' feet"; the female license simply authorized a woman to "do all the work that may devolve on her as a prophetess or FEMALE MINISTER of the gospel."[47]

Prominent Early Pentecostal Women

Several outstanding women in the early movement had ministries rivaling those of more touted male colleagues. Despite exclusion by some denominational limitations, women were in demand as speakers and revivalists. Several women were instrumental in forming the lives and ministries of males, who more easily found their way into Pentecostal historiography.

One of the earliest and most famous Pentecostal women preachers and evangelists of her time was faith healer Maria

Woodworth Etter. She had been prominent on the late-nineteenth-century Holiness camp meeting circuit for many years, holding meetings that regularly drew thousands, and was the only prominent Holiness faith healer to accept the Pentecostal message. She began preaching in 1880, and, years before the Azusa Street Revival, many elements of Pentecostalism were evident in her meetings, including healing, exorcism, miracles, glossolalia, trances, visions, and people being "slain in the Spirit." Etter held her largest revivals between 1912 and 1913, when she was nearly seventy years of age. Attendance at many of her meetings regularly ran in the thousands.

More than one reportedly drew more than twenty-five thousand people. Although primarily an evangelist, she was also a prolific church planter who organized congregations throughout her ministry. Her method was to preach a series of meetings in a community, organize the converts, and place someone in charge of the new congregation. Although we do not know how many congregations Etter established, by the end of a single one-and-one-half-year period of ministry, she had preached nine revivals and organized two congregations—one with more than seventy members. In 1918, although still traveling and evangelizing, Etter founded the only church she pastored, the Woodworth-Etter Tabernacle in Indianapolis. Since she never organized the many congregations she started into a denomination or affiliated with an existing denomination, many of her followers later joined the Assemblies of God, and after her death Woodworth-Etter Tabernacle also affiliated with that body.[48]

As a committed biblical feminist who defended women's right to preach and encouraged them to go into the ministry, at one point she insisted, "It is high time for women to let their lights shine, to bring out their talents that have been hidden away rusting, and use them for the glory of God."[49]

27

Another woman whose more than sixty years of ministry—from 1880 to 1946—bridged both the Holiness and Pentecostal movements was Carrie Judd Montgomery. At nineteen, she experienced a debilitating spinal fever from which she was miraculously, instantaneously healed. Her healing and testimony caught the attention of her Buffalo, New York, community and set her on a mission of writing and speaking about divine healing. Around 1880, at age twenty-two, she wrote her first book, The Prayer of Faith, which was translated into four languages. In 1881, she began to publish Triumphs of Faith: A Monthly Journal for the Promotion of Healing and Holiness. Montgomery wrote many tracts on the themes of healing and holiness and continued to publish the magazine for sixty-six years, until her death. Following her miraculous healing, her family set up her sick room as a "faith sanctuary." In 1882, they established Faith Rest Cottage in Buffalo and Carrie became involved in leading a network of faith homes in western New York.

After moving to California and marrying well-to-do businessman, George Montgomery, who provided financial support for her ministry, she established a faith home, House of Peace, to provide respite for missionaries from more than one hundred mission boards. Within the home, she established Beulah Chapel and served as pastor for its weekly worship services. She also founded Shalom Training School for Missionaries, a children's home for orphans, and an annual camp meeting at Cazadera, California.[50]

Montgomery associated with many prominent Holiness leaders, including the hymnist William Broadman, A. B. Simpson of the Christian and Missionary Alliance, and William and Catherine Booth, founders of the Salvation Army. She had been active in the Christian and Missionary Alliance until she received the Pentecostal baptism of the Holy Spirit, and even after that time , she never broke fellowship with the group, but continued her steady preaching schedule—now adding the Pentecostal message to her theology. In 1909, she and her husband embarked on a missionary trip around the world, traveling to Japan, China, India, and England. Montgomery was a charter member of the General Council of the Assemblies of God from 1914, having joined with the group when it was part of the Church of God in Christ.[51]

Marie Burgess was baptized in the Holy Spirit in 1906 under Charles Parham's ministry in Alexander Dowie's religious community at Zion City, Illinois. Almost immediately, she began preaching, moving from Illinois to Michigan, and then to Ohio, before Parham sent her to New York City to evangelize in 1907. In that same year, she set up Glad Tidings Hall Apostolic Faith Mission in the heart of Manhattan. In 1909, she married Robert Brown, and the two guided the church to becoming Glad Tidings Tabernacle, for a long time the most prominent Pentecostal Church in New York City and on the East Coast. After the marriage, however, Marie took a subordinate role to her husband in the leadership of the congregation. In 1917, the church affiliated with the Assemblies of God and Robert took on a leadership role in the denomination. After Robert's death in 1948, Marie continued as senior pastor until her death in 1971.

One of the most fruitful early Pentecostal missionaries was Lillian Trasher, whose fifty-one-year ministry in Egypt was so successful that two major Pentecostal bodies celebrate her accomplishments. Beginning in 1910, until her death in 1961, she first worked under her own auspices, then with the Church of God, and finally with the Assemblies of God. Though licensed with the former body from 1912 to 1919, Trasher received only limited financial support from the denomination for a ministry that had already begun to show signs that it would be significant. Yet, one historian credits her with being the first Church of God foreign missionary. Her ministry was largely to children and women, and she initially housed orphans and homeless

29

and abused women in her own home. By 1916, she was housing fifty orphans there. Trasher built and operated the first building of a permanent home for orphans and women from a donation from a group of wealthy Coptic supporters. By the time she died, the orphanage had expanded to thirteen buildings, including a church, a clinic, and an elementary school, and she was revered by the Egyptian leaders and community.[52]

The Decline in Women's Leadership

Barfoot and Sheppard's work on the ministry of women in early Pentecostalism places the beginning of the decline of women's leadership after World War 1.[53] They rightly attribute the decline, in part, to the evolution from a prophetic to a priestly movement. As a prophetic movement, Pentecostalism anticipated the imminent return of Christ and sought to enlist everyone to preach the gospel to a world that was otherwise doomed. It was eager to reach all who were lost, without adopting the institutional trappings of gender stratification and denominational hierarchy. They contend that later, as part of a priestly movement, realizing that Christ's return might be delayed, Pentecostal leaders sought to bring order to a church that might have to endure for several years.[54] Although Pentecostal women's leadership h been in a tenuous state from the very beginning, it became even more limited. Again, however, the degree of restriction varied, depending on the sect or denomination.

Letha Scanzoni and Susan Setta rightly identify the beginning of the decline as occurring much earlier in the movement. They see the motions for decline being in place at the movement's inception with the incorporation of "limited restrictions" that resulted in only "limited equality, or what I call "limited liberty.""[55] They also identify the ambivalence regarding the issue of the public ministry of women that was part of the ethos of the movement. For example, many Pentecostals understood a woman as being able to be a "spiritual leader" at church but under her husband's leadership at home. Another ambivalent understanding held that women were God's second choice, employed only when a man was not available for a specific ministry.[56]

Many Pentecostal women accepted these understandings and the restrictions that came with them. For one reason, as Scanzoni and Setta point out, women who acquiesced to these tenets fared better among their male colleagues than those who were outspoken.[57] Such notable women as McPherson and Tate took no public stand on the position of women in the church and society unless they were pushed to do so. They generally responded only when their own ministry was directly called into question in relation to gender issues.

What started as small limitations on women's ministry slowly became severe restrictions. As several factors limited that initial liberty, several contributed to further decline. First, the eschatological, premillennial hope of Christ's imminent return waned with the realization that several years had passed and Jesus had not come. With fading hope of an immediate parousia, Pentecostal anti denominational, anti-structural bias gave way to the realization that the movement needed some organization if it was to last until Christ returned. Loosely tied sects began to form denominations with written polity and doctrine. From the beginning, some restrictions on women's ministry and leadership were generally incorporated into these polities.

With more pronounced structure came what Edith Blumhofer describes as a growing "professionalization" of the ministry. One characteristic of this, according to Blumhofer, was differing criteria for credentialing men and women, exemplified in hierarchical ranks of ministry with dual tracks for women and men. Another was the move of ministry from a primarily voluntary vocation to a paid occupation— at least for men.[58] Barfoot and Sheppard characterize it as Pentecostal bodies seeking to pattern themselves after major Protestant denominations.[59] With these restrictions in place, women were cognizant of limits on their ministries long before World War II. Yet, they persisted in entering the ministry in large numbers and seeking

31

leadership roles. As Barfoot and Sheppard graphically detail, however, with increased restrictions, the actual numbers of women who answered the call and pursued public ministry and leadership "declined annually."[60]

Conclusion

In 1908, five years after Mary Magdalena Tate planted her first congregation, one year after Florence Crawford founded her first congregation, and two years into the life of the Azusa Street Revival, Pentecostal women were playing a vibrant, though somewhat restricted, role in the movement. They were preaching, teaching, establishing churches, serving as missionaries, and following the dictates of their God-inspired calls. There was a general sense of expectation and urgency that compelled all who felt called to get involved in the ministry of the gospel.

By 1923, a year before Ida Robinson launched the Mt. Sinai Holy Church of America and two years before Aimee Semple McPherson started building Angeles Temple, the restrictions on women's ministry had begun in earnest within the major Pentecostal denominations. By 1925, when Robinson's denomination was holding its first convocation and electing her presiding bishop, the Church of God, in which she had previously served, had stripped women of most of their ministerial rights including voting in business meetings of their own congregations, performing sacraments, and voting in the General Assembly, its governing body.

While the movement was in its embryonic stages, women enjoyed the greatest liberty, though it was somewhat limited. From the time that the loose sects began to organize into denominations, restrictions on the leadership and ministry of women grew. Generally, women worked within these limitations to carry out their ministries, and despite them were relatively effective in doing so. A few women, however, found even these "limited restrictions" untenable.

Florence Louise Crawford
Apostolic Faith Church

During the infancy of the modern Pentecostal movement, a woman with a very unlikely spiritual heritage came to play an important role. As a participant and leader of the Azusa Street Revival, Florence Louise Crawford helped shape this event and carry its message throughout the Pacific Northwest. After attending the early stages of the revival, she rose to a position of trust and importance and was one of the original six female members of the Azusa Street Mission administrative board. She initially served faithfully in a variety of ministries at the mission.

Like many who felt a strong evangelistic pull, her involvement with the revival was short-lived. Within several months Crawford had moved on to start her own ministry. Leaving from there, she was among the first women—or men—to take the Pentecostal message outside the revival, carrying it to the Pacific Northwest, and among the earliest to form a denomination. In so doing, Crawford became the woman from the Azusa Street Revival who had the widest influence beyond the initial period of the Pentecostal movement. [1]

Early Life And Ministry
Florence Reed was born in September 1872 in Coos County in western Oregon. She was one of ten children of Oscar and Mary Reed, both of whom had come to the region with their respective parents, as children, by covered wagon. Although both parents eventually came to faith, during her childhood they were atheists who regularly hosted free thinkers in their home for lectures and discussions. From an early age, Florence was privy to these exchanges, regularly hearing scripture discounted and attacked. The family's library held books by prominent thinkers and regularly the Reeds read to their children from these

works "as Christians read from the Bible." Although nothing is known of Crawford's formal education, in the frontier environment in which she lived, a high level of formal schooling would have been rare. Yet she certainly was exposed to a breadth of intellectual material. Her later achievement showed evidence of having the sharp mind to grasp it.

Often, her parents' guests would soundly deny the existence of God as well as the deity of Christ. After her conversion, Crawford insisted that even back then, "something way down in my heart would say, 'I know there is a God.' He would not let me believe what those men were saying."2 Still, in her childhood, Florence was not exposed to Christian values and, "never laid hands on an actual Bible until... a grown woman."3 She appeared, however, to have had an early interest in religious concerns. How this came about is uncertain, yet two incidences in her young life are indicative. Once, as a child, Florence sneaked off to a camp meeting where she was deeply touched by the singing and message. From that time, she "longed for something in my heart that I did not have... and did not know what it was."4 On another occasion, probably when she was a young teen, her family hosted a famous free thinker as a lecturer in their home. Florence was asked to sing a solo and chose to sing, "Jesus, Lover of My Soul." By the time she finished her selection, several were in tears, having been visibly moved by the fervor with which she sang. At that time, she had yet not made a confession of Christian faith.

Despite somewhat poor health, young Florence led an active life, frequenting theaters, hosting card parties, and engaging in ballroom dancing. But social activities were not all that took her attention. After settling in California, she became active in social outreach work and activist issues. These interests, along with her leadership abilities, led her to serve terms as president of the Los Angeles and state chapters of the Women's Christian Temperance League. In 1902, she also served as the first president of the Los Angeles chapter of the National

Congress of Mothers. The organization later became the Parent-Teacher Association (PTA).

Notwithstanding her lack of early exposure to the Christian faith, Crawford's Christian experience began dramatically and seemingly came out of nowhere, when she had what she characterized as a direct confrontation with God in what would seem to most a very unlikely place, a ballroom dance floor. She recalled the episode:

> One night as I was dancing in a ballroom I heard a voice speak out of Heaven and say, "Daughter, give Me thine heart." I did not know it was the voice of God so I went on dancing. Again the voice spoke. It seemed my feet became heavy and the place was no longer beautiful to me. Again the voice spoke much louder," Daughter, give Me thine heart!" The music died away and I left the ballroom; and for three days and nights I prayed and wept, wrestling against the powers of atheism and dark-ness. The enemy would tell me there was no God, and that the Bible was a myth. I could hardly eat or sleep, and it seemed there was no hope for me, but I thought: Why did God speak out of Heaven if there were no hope?

> Finally I remembered a little woman who was a Christian,... and I went to her home. When she opened the door and looked at my face she said, "You want God." I said, "I want Him more than anything else in the world." Right there I fell on my knees, and as she prayed for me, God came into my heart[5]

Once converted, Crawford transferred her enthusiasm for social outreach to her church work. In 1890, she traveled from Oregon to Los Angeles. Very shortly after arriving in the city, she approached the juvenile court and the prison warden for permission to work with inmates. She carried on weekly worship services at the city jail and established a harness shop to train men released from jail and help them establish a work record and reference for use in seeking permanent employment.[6]

Within a year, she was married to a building contractor, Frank Mortimer Crawford. The couple had two children- Raymond, born in 1891, and Mildred, born in 1896. Sometime later, they adopted a girl named Virginia. The marriage was not particularly successful and, after seventeen years, the couple separated. But final dissolution of the marriage may have had more to do with Florence's newly formed theology than with an unhappy situation at home.

During the seventeen years between arriving in Los Angeles and coming to the Azusa Street Revival, Crawford affiliated with several congregations, including those of Methodists, Presbyterians, and Christian and Missionary Alliance, searching for a religious environment that would nurture her newfound faith. Her earliest connection was with the First Methodist Church, where her leadership skills and spiritual fervor landed her a position as a class leader. Soon, however, an issue arose when she asked to be baptized. She and the pastor differed on the baptismal mode; he suggesting sprinkling and she insisting on immersion. When he would not relent, Florence left the congregation.

None of these early involvements completely satisfied Crawford, who was searching for the experience of sanctification- the inner assurance that she had attained sinless perfection as a fit vessel for God's use. Advisors suggested the pursuit was fruitless and exhorted her to accept, by faith, that she had received it. Despite such

37

exhortation, Crawford eventually ended up at the New Testament Church congregation of Holiness pastor William Smale, former pastor of the city's First Baptist Church. Involvement with Smale's group only whetted her appetite for a still deeper spiritual experience, and so her pursuit intensified. As she put it:

> One day I stood on the corner of Fifth and Main Streets, in Los Angeles, California. God had saved me. I was doing my rescue work to keep, it seemed, the little fire in my heart fanned to a flame. I had been in this church and that one. I stood there that day, my heart aching. I said, "Is there no place where they believe the whole Word?" I would not exchange for anything in the whole world that hunger that God planted in my heart which searched and sought until at last I found them.[7]

That search for a group who wholeheartedly embraced this understanding led Crawford to the Azusa Street Mission during the early days of the revival. Yet, despite the progressive ideas Crawford's family had espoused, they held the common racial prejudices of the day, and previously she and her husband had "looked down on any one who even spoke to a colored [sic] person, unless he was a servant." But Crawford was so hungry for that deeper spiritual experience that she pushed past her racial prejudice. At first, however, she did not allow her family to know that she was attending services with blacks.[8]

Her hunger for the experience was so strong that, once she overcame her racial prejudice, she not only received sanctification, but three days later, the baptism of the Holy Spirit. Indeed, she contended that she was the first white women to receive the Pentecostal experience once the meeting moved to Azusa Street. With the ability to speak in tongues in what a Chinese member of the congregation identified as fluent Chinese, Crawford was also able to write in tongues and reportedly wrote seven or eight different languages.[9]

At the same time Crawford received the Pentecostal experience, she reportedly was instantaneously healed from ailments that had plagued her for years. As a child, she had had three episodes of spinal meningitis, which left her with poor eyesight. As a young teen she had been thrown from a carriage and incurred a back injury that required her to wear surgical supports for eleven years. An earlier bout with tuberculosis had left her with a chronic cough and hemorrhaging.[10] She recounted the miraculous healing that affected every part of her body:

I had many afflictions until God baptized me with the Holy Ghost and fire. I had worn glasses for years... and... could not leave the glasses off. I went to the mission that afternoon and told what wonderful things the Lord had done for me. As I had them pray, the healing power of the Son of God flowed through my eyes, and my eyes were perfect. I had lung trouble for years and had to live in southern California for my health, but God healed me of that. I was thin, diseased, broken down in every part of my body, but when I had paid the full price and in simple, childlike faith prayed that I might get my health back again and be a witness for Him in this world, the healing streams began to flow.[11]

Prior to coming to Azusa Street, Crawford had promised God that, if he would heal her, she would dedicate her life to preaching the gospel. Once the healing occurred, Crawford began to play an increasingly important role in the revival. Along with serving on the administrative team, during the worship services she could be found working at the altar, praying for those who needed healing or wanted salvation, sanctification, or the baptism of the Holy Spirit.

As co-editor (along with Seymour) of *The Apostolic Faith*, Crawford was second only to Seymour in the number of signed articles found in its pages. She was instrumental in distributing the periodical, and the extent of her influence among the revival's constituents can be attested by the fact that in later editions of the newsletter, she, like Seymour, had resorted to using only her initials to sign articles. The assumption is that everyone knew who F. L. C. was. Her faithful service led Seymour to appoint her to the ministry within four months of her arriving at Azusa Street. Perhaps in admiration of her tenacity, he named her state overseer of California. In this role, she oversaw evangelism and missionary efforts throughout the state and was responsible for opening new works throughout the state in the name of the Apostolic Faith Mission.

Crawford was known for having visions that she often relayed in a testimony service or to the readers of *The Apostolic Faith*:

> While Sister Crawford was praying for money to send workers to Oakland, the Lord gave her a vision of three bills she would receive and she received three five-dollar bills. Then when praying about her fare to Salem, Oregon, she saw three gold pieces and sure enough she received the gold pieces.[12]

A shorter item in the same issue simply said, "Sister Florence Crawford says she had a vision of a beautiful bouquet of flowers all in the bud, and the Lord said to her, 'This movement is just in the bud.'"[13]

Establishing The Apostolic Faith Mission

But though Crawford loved the spiritual atmosphere she found at the revival she would not stay at the Azusa Street Mission for long. Within several months of her arrival, she was anxious to hit the evangelistic circuit, responding to what she felt was a call of God.

Sister Florence Crawford says: "There is no spot on earth so dear to me as this place, but I must go out and tell this story. Souls are perishing far and near. The Lord told me yesterday to go into all the world and preach His Gospel. 'The kingdom of heaven is at hand,' and 'Behold, I come quickly.' What He says to me, He says to every baptized soul. He wants us to go out into the highways and hedges and declare this Gospel. He has anointed me to tell the story of Jesus and I can go alone, for Jesus is with me. O, glory to God!"[14]

Within a few months of her Pentecostal experience, Crawford embarked on an evangelistic campaign. She was among the first missionaries to go out from Azusa Street to take the message of the revival to other communities. Like most of the others who fanned out from the revival, Crawford had no financial backing from the mission. Instead, like those others, she went solely "by faith," counting on offerings from the various churches in which she preached to sustain her and ultimately trusting that God would somehow provide for her personal needs and those of the ministry in God's time and manner.

She went first with a team that included G. W. and May Evans, Ophelia Wiley, Lulu Miller, and Thomas Junk and his wife[15] to Oakland, California, and held a revival at William Manley's Household of Faith. During that meeting, reportedly "sixty-five souls received the baptism with the Holy Ghost, thirty were sanctified, and nineteen converted."[16] Although at first this was only to be a short trip, Crawford stayed there for five weeks.

While in Oakland, she traveled across the bay to San Francisco on at least one occasion to hold revival meetings. In December she wrote back to the Azusa Street Mission:

41

I was in San Francisco last night, and such a meeting we had. I never saw such sweet unity of the Spirit-testimony, healing, singing in the Holy Ghost, praying for the sick, and some receiving their Pentecost at the same time, and no confusion.

O it was glorious and surely the Holy Ghost led the meeting. As I read the text or lesson about bridling the tongue, a dear brother that has been a power in mission work, healing the sick and preaching, said, "Pray for me now that my tongue may be bridled." The power came for prayer, I laid hands on him and he was baptized and spoke in such a clear language.

Another preacher was baptized soon after. O God is working mightily!

A man was completely healed of rupture of nine years' standing, last night. O how can we praise Him enough. A sister the first time in the meeting was healed and anointed, went home and got her Pentecost the same night. God is working where He has a chance. O for closer walk with Him. I don't know when I shall get home, but where Jesus is 'tis heaven. O how my full heart does praise Him.[17]

The next stop for Crawford and the team was Salem, Oregon, where pastor M. L. Ryan invited her to conduct a series of meetings. Ryan, a Holiness pastor, had visited Azusa Street, received the Holy Ghost, and subsequently requested that someone come from Los Angeles to help his congregation. Before Crawford arrived, Ryan had alerted the press that he expected a group from the now famous Azusa Street Revival and announced their impending arrival in his publication, Light. The meetings drew people from throughout the Pacific Northwest, including Portland and its surrounding communities. Although highly anticipated by the faithful, these meetings stirred up controversy among the larger religious community, partly because of Crawford's public assertion that she was able not only to speak, but also to write, in tongues. This practice was not endorsed by the Azusa Street Mission, but it had been part of the experience of some in Parham's group in Topeka, Kansas. Ryan himself engaged in the practice, and greater notoriety was drawn to the practice when he insisted that Jesus was left-handed.

One of the people attending the Salem meetings was the wife of an African American pastor from Portland, John Glasco. After hearing Crawford speak and experiencing her ministry, Mrs. Glasco invited her to come to Portland to conduct similar meetings that she expected would help her husband's fledgling congregation. Crawford arrived in Portland at noon on Christmas Day, 1906, only eight months after the Azusa Street Revival had begun. Three hours later she was holding her first revival service at Glasco's St. John Gospel Mission. Later that evening she held a second service. Reminiscent of the Azusa Street Revival, the congregation met in a former blacksmith shop that had been converted into a sanctuary.

By Crawford's account, the revival was a spiritual success. During the week, she filed a report back to the Los Angeles congregation that crowds were filling the hall each night—every chair was filled, the aisles were packed, the doorway was jammed, and people who could not get in stood out in the street. She also indicated that city officials expressed concern that the meeting posed a fire hazard and took measures to limit the number of people entering the place.

Each night, when the invitation to prayer was given, there were so many who wanted to pray that it was difficult to find room at the altar or elsewhere. All available kneeling space was quickly taken, and

43

sometimes the doors had to be locked in order to keep the crowds away who might disturb those seeking God in prayer. By the time the meeting ended several weeks later, a number of people had had the Pentecostal experience of speaking in tongues, and Crawford was firmly established as an evangelistic preacher with a powerful Pentecostal message.

Crawford returned to Los Angeles for three months, then went out again on the evangelistic circuit, again going to Portland, Oregon, then to Seattle, Washington. She then went east to Minnesota and up to Canada. In Minneapolis, God spoke to her and told her to establish the headquarters for her ministry in Portland, Oregon. Indeed, she felt that God was intending to make her Portland work "the center of the Apostolic Faith work."[18]

Seymour was at first reluctant for Crawford to leave the mission, for reasons that are not initially clear. Eventually, however, she and Seymour disagreed on two, at first seemingly distant, issues: his decision to marry and his purported compromise on the matter of holiness. The disagreement over his decision to marry stemmed from two possible sources. First, Crawford held the same radical understanding of Christ's imminent return to which many early Pentecostals adhered. Although she herself was married, she left her husband, having come to the extreme position some held that such normal activities as marriage and raising a family were counterproductive to the urgent need to reach as many as possible with the Pentecostal message before Christ's return. Second, since Crawford had held a somewhat prominent place in the ministry, she may have felt threatened by what the new alliance between Seymour and Jennie Evans Moore could mean for her own leadership position. At any rate, Crawford left Los Angeles and moved to Portland to set up her own Apostolic Faith Church.

Another possible contributor to the breach might have been the loyalty Crawford felt to Clara Lum. Crawford and Lum had worked closely with Seymour in producing *The Apostolic Faith*. The two women developed a friendship during this period, possibly because of their shared interest and experience in rescue home work. Lum and Seymour's relationship apparently had a deeper quality to it. Reportedly, both had entertained the idea that the friendship could grow into a relationship that might result in marriage. But because Lum was white and Seymour black, Seymour was cautioned against such a marriage because of the controversy that would surely ensue and the repercussions to the ministry.[19] It is not surprising, then, that Lum, like Crawford, objected to Seymour's decision to marry Jennie Evans Moore. After the marriage, Lum left the mission to join Crawford. She never married.

At any rate, Crawford felt the marriage and other stances taken by Seymour signaled compromise on the issue of holiness or sanctification. But also, by this time, Seymour had begun to institute a number of small, but significant, changes to the government of the Azusa Street Mission that would limit the level of leadership to which Crawford, as a woman, could ultimately rise. At some point in developing a doctrinal statement for the mission, Seymour clearly distinguished the roles men and women were to play in worship and ministry leadership. He insisted that "all ordination must be done by men-not women. Women [could] be ministers but not... baptize or ordain in this work."[20] The ordination liturgy he developed indicates that all laying on of hands and prayer in such services were to be done by "elders." Already ranks of ministry to which women might aspire were limited such that the ranks of elder and then bishop were restricted to men; women were relegated to lower ranks with less ministerial privilege. For Crawford, who was accustomed to serving in

45

high ranks of secular leadership, such a limitation must have proven unacceptable.

So, in spite of objections from Seymour and from Crawford's own husband, she had left the Azusa Street Mission for Portland. Pastor Glasco offered Crawford leadership of his congregation, which she accepted with the stipulation that she could run the church according to her convictions. These included the immediate suspension of all formal collection of money. Instead, Crawford insisted that the congregation be supported solely on faith and on the unsolicited generosity of those who attended services. To facilitate giving, a collection box was placed at the door; even today, though the organization upholds that tithing is the biblical model for giving, no formal offering is ever taken.

By June, Crawford had secured a site and held a series of tent revival camp meetings. Partly because of the general excitement that the new Pentecostal movement was generating and partly because of her charismatic style, Crawford's ministry grew rapidly. By the end of the meeting, the congregation had grown to such an extent that it was necessary to move to larger permanent quarters. In September 1907, only five months after moving to Portland, Crawford purchased the first building for her organization. She also contacted the Apostolic Faith Missions that she had helped launch while working under Seymour to let them know of her move and solicit their support for her new endeavor. Several congregations joined with her and severed their ties with Seymour. By October 1909, the Apostolic Faith Missionwas a registered religious organization in the state of Oregon.

As was true regarding many early Pentecostals, the surrounding community found it hard to wholeheartedly accept Crawford's revivals, and she suffered both derision and persecution. Members of the area press launched attacks that depicted her and her meetings as rowdy, obnoxious, and uncouth. Mobs attacked the ministry from time to

46

time, lobbing rotten vegetables and other missiles at the premises. They frequently caused damage to the camp meeting tents or church building. At one point, the glass in all of the windows and doors of the new facility was broken. Crawford herself came under physical and emotional attack. During one meeting, an attempt was made to arrest her. In another, she was cut in the face by a bottle hurled at her.

Yet, as Crawford saw it, her meetings were tame compared to many Pentecostal revivals of that time. She rigidly controlled the spiritual demonstrations of those in attendance and was later to recount that in her meetings,

> there was "[n]o fanaticism or fleshly demonstrations....
> These were not allowed. Many people have come here and say, 'We don't see the manifestations we expected.' Well, you will see the Power of God! If there are any manifestations, they will be the genuine kind, if you get an experience here."[21]

In addition to what outsiders still saw as the frenetic worship characteristic of early Pentecostal meetings, Crawford's ministry provided another target for attack. The congregation that she took over was largely African American, and from the time she assumed its leadership. Her meetings exhibited the interracial Pentecostal ethos to an extent that was problematic even in the Pacific Northwest. In a suit brought against Crawford by Portland's juvenile court for lack of appropriate supervision of her daughter Mildred, one of the chief complaints was that she allowed her to be a part of "fantastic orgies of blacks and whites." To this day, the commitment of the Apostolic Faith Church to diversity among its constituents and leadership is unprecedented among Pentecostal denominations.

Even with such criticism, within the Pentecostal circles in which she now found herself, Crawford was considered a powerful woman of spirit and her meetings were counted a success. Even within the secular community, Crawford's group eventually gained a degree of respect from city officials, who came to recognize the change that her ministry had caused in the lives of some of their less desirable citizens.

Over the nearly thirty years she headed the denomination, Crawford's ministry was focused heavily on evangelism, and she used every tool available to reach and win as many as possible to the Pentecostal faith. In April 1908, she published the first Portland issue of *The Apostolic Faith* and by July of that year, the city had become the newspaper's international publishing headquarters. Just how that came to be is a greatly disputed. The Apostolic Faith Church still maintains that she was asked by the Azusa Street Mission to take over publication of the paper, so she brought that work and the mailing list with her.[22]

With her 1908 move, the Azusa Street ministry turned over two of the existing twenty-two copies of the mailing list, and transferred the responsibility of publishing paper to her. Though published in Los Angeles after the move, the May issue contained the note: "For the next issues of this paper address The Apostolic Faith Camp meeting, Portland, Oregon."[23]

Some suggest that Crawford's departure and the moving of the mailing list had a less friendly unfolding. They, like Seymour, contend that Crawford and her followers removed the newspaper operations without consent. Perhaps more important than movement of the mailing list was relocation of the expertise for editing and publishing a newsletter, largely lodged with Clara Lum and Florence Crawford, who were among the few Azusa Street faithful able to pull off such an operation. At any rate, once the newspaper moved to Oregon, Crawford raised the English language production rate to one hundred fifty thousand bi-monthly issues. In 1908, that same year, a German

48

edition, Apostoliche Glaube, and a Norwegian edition, Den Apostoliske Tro, were published. Seymour made several attempts to get the mailing list back from Crawford, but failed. As a result, the relationship between the two remained contentious for several years. During that period, Seymour also made at least one failed attempt to gain control of Crawford's work, and Crawford, in return, opened a rival congregation in Los Angeles and convinced a number of congregations that Seymour's group had started with her assistance to transfer their allegiance to her organization. [24]

Beyond her initial effort with *The Apostolic Faith* newspaper, Crawford aggressively used print media to promote her vision. By 1917, the organization began installing its own equipment in a new publishing house, and by 1919, brought printing of paper in-house. It soon added new editions, including a children's edition, The Armor Bearer, and a special edition for prison work. In addition, the publishing house printed tracts, Sunday school materials, and other ministry resources.

Crawford's evangelistic ingenuity was showcased in the innovative means she used to spread the message of the Apostolic Faith Church. She graduated from horse-drawn wagons in the early days (considered the most modern means of transportation available to the common person), and she continued to employ ever new modes. Motorboats, automobiles, and airplanes were still relatively new modes of transport, yet she employed them to carry her message by land, sea, and air to anyone who would listen. In 1915, a team of people from the Apostolic Faith launched a transcontinental evangelistic automobile tour across the United States, stopping in large cities and many smaller towns and communities.

Motorboats began to be used in outreach to foreign sailors on merchant ships in Portland Harbor in 1913. Between that time and 1925, two additional boats were added to the fleet. In 1919, during the

49

infancy of aviation, Crawford purchased the first gospel plane, the Sky Pilot, to drop religious tracts and revival announcements over cities in the Pacific Northwest. Nine years later, in 1928, a second plane, the Wings of the Morning, was purchased.[25] The medium of radio evangelism was incorporated into Crawford's ministry beginning in 1934 with a broadcast that reached throughout the Portland area. But she did not overlook simpler media. She took pains to stay connected not just to the larger world, but to the individuals who needed her attention. In the early days of the ministry Crawford gave personal attention to the hundreds of pieces of correspondence the Apostolic Faith Church regularly received from around the world, reading many of them herself, and often dictating personal responses. Instead of a form letter, writers received a reply tailored to their situations. In one case she wrote to someone in need of prayer for healing: "Take new hope and courage... look forward to the coming of the Lord, which will do more for you than anything else. I have prayed for you, suffered with you, and believe that God is going to raise you up and that you will yet be able to work for the Master and have some sheaves to lay at his feet."[26]

When Crawford first arrived in Portland, she again took up her passion for prison ministry and began holding regular worship services in the Multnomah County Jail. This passion remained an integral part of her ministry. During her lifetime, she continued to visit prisons throughout the area and encouraged congregations in other locations to do the same.

Crawford's secular upbringing gave her an appreciation for music and other artistic forms that found their way into the ministry of the Apostolic Faith. As a result, music has always been an integral part of the spiritual atmosphere of the church. Crawford composed several hymns and encouraged others within her movement to do so. After her death, the denomination collected the hymns of several Apostolic

50

Faith composers, including her son and daughter, into a denominational hymnal.

By 1913, only six years after she formed the first Portland congregation, Crawford began putting an extensive music program in place. By 1922 the church had a twenty-two-piece orchestra. By 1932, her congregation was known in the Portland community for its annual musical concerts, which regularly drew thousands and featured the orchestra and choir performing original pieces along with Christian standards.

Theologically, Crawford placed herself solidly among the mainstream of classical Holiness-Pentecostals and condemned what she considered extreme formulations. For her, sanctification was a core of this theology. She, like most early Pentecostals, held to a rigid personal piety that included strictures concerning women's apparel and restrictions on believer 's social relationships and activities with unbelievers. But Crawford went even farther. As she saw it, the condition of being unspotted called for drastic measures, including forbidding remarriage as long as either partner had a living former spouse. It further required remarried couples who wanted to join the Apostolic Faith Church to separate from their new mate, renounce the second marriage, and the partners return to the original mates. One issue of *The Apostolic Faith* declared, "Many are living with someone else's wife or husband. They say they are justified by the law of the land, but they are not justified by the Law of God. God demands that you restore what you have stolen and make your life straight."[27]

For Crawford and her church, the insistence on restitution was a core of true repentance. This stance was a carryover from Seymour's Azusa Street Mission, yet whether Seymour, Crawford, or someone else was the originator is unclear. The implications of rigid adherence to this tenant were widespread and had both positive and negative effects. Newly converted spouses (generally husbands) returned to

51

their abandoned families to take up their rightful place as the head, restoring these families to what Crawford saw as biblical order. Sometimes, however, this meant that women who joined or remained in the church were counseled to stay in unloving or even abusive marriages for the sake of maintaining what was seen as a biblically ordered home.[28]

A 1935 *Time Magazine* article suggested that Crawford held even more radical ideas-frowning on marriage entirely, counseling young people to stay single, and encouraging celibacy among those who were married.[29] For Crawford, this did not appear to be a spiritual consideration in which sexual intercourse was seen as impure. Rather it was a practical consideration in which such mundane activity was seen as interfering with the business of saving as many souls as possible before the imminent return of Jesus.

The Time article referred to Crawford as "twice-married"—a term that would have sounded strange to many of those who knew her. But reportedly, sometime in her late teens, while still living in Oregon, Florence had married John Hammersly. The couple had no children and that marriage had ended in divorce before Florence was eighteen.[30] Most biographical information regarding Crawford overlooks this short interlude, and the 1935 article is the only written resource that alludes to the fact that she had been married more than once.[31] But once Crawford became convinced of the unbiblical foundation for the validity of a second marriage, she made herself subject to this understanding.

One of the seemingly harshest strictures was the prohibition against participating in worship services and religious functions with other groups-even other Pentecostal groups. Since Crawford felt that many of these other groups did not go far enough in upholding the doctrine or practical application of sanctification, she felt that involvement with them would influence her followers to compromise their own standards on these issues.

She subscribed to the teaching regarding divine healing and made prayer for healing a regular part of her ministry. In part, this commitment to divine healing was colored by her experience of having been healed from a number of serious ailments. Further, she had experienced what she considered a direct response to prayer for healing from a condition that hampered the breathing of her daughter, Mildred.

But Crawford added several elements unique to her theological mindset in preaching her "Latter Rain Gospel." First, while placing a heavy emphasis on the biblical mandate for tithing, she refused to collect a formal offering. Crawford upheld giving one-tenth of an individual's income as a biblically sanctioned pattern for giving, but members were expected to do this without prompting. Further, Crawford's congregations and denomination have no formal membership. This policy remains in force within the organization today and is one reason statistics on adherents are difficult to assess.

Throughout her tenure as head of the denomination, three people worked closely with Crawford: Clara Lum, William Trotter, and Crawford's son, Raymond. All three proved indispensable in helping Crawford carry out her vision. Outside of a few anecdotal glimpses, however, little is known of the quality of the personal relationships she shared with them.

Before coming to Azusa Street, Clara Lum had been a servant in William Parham's home and had edited The Firebrand, the newspaper of Charles Hanley's World's Faith Missionary Association. She arrived at the revival with several years of experience as a Holiness preacher, specifically seeking the baptism of the Holy Spirit. After receiving it, she served on the mission's governing board and participated in various aspects of the worship service, where she exercised the gifts of tongues and interpretation and read the testimonies of those who wrote in. Because of her clerical and administrative skills, she recorded the messages in tongues given at the revival, and she served as secretary and co-editor (along with Seymour) of *The Apostolic Faith* from 1906 to 1908.

Lum, like Crawford, had objected to Seymour's marriage, left the mission, and moved to Oregon, corroborating with Crawford in taking the mailing list. After coming to the city, the two began republishing the newspaper, Lum serving as its editor, as well as editor of the children's newsletter, The Armor Bearer. She also served as a teacher in the Apostolic Faith School.

William Trotter had been superintendent of the Union Rescue Mission of Los Angeles and was first recruited by Crawford to work with her evangelistic efforts on behalf of Seymour's mission. When he became involved in the Pentecostal movement and announced to his board that he had received the experience of speaking in tongues, he was asked to resign. Subsequently, Crawford invited him to work with her in conducting campaigns throughout California.

Trotter was very influential in his own right, enjoying friendships with such important people as Christian philanthropist Lyman Stewart, founder of Union Oil Company, and his brother, Milton. The relationship with the Stewarts served as a valuable resource for raising support for causes that were important to Trotter. These included help for the Gospel Mission where Trotter served. His support was also vital for founding the Bible Institute of Los Angeles that later became Biola University. Once Trotter was dismissed from the mission, Stewart continued his friendship and the financial support of Trotter's ministry efforts, including those carried out on behalf of Crawford.

Once Crawford moved her organization to Portland, Trotter became her chief lieutenant. During the ten years he served with Crawford, the two drew on their extensive rescue work experience to support their aggressive outreach effort, and Trotter again became engaged in rescue mission work-this time in the name of the Apostolic Faith Mission. He also shared with Crawford pastoral and preaching responsibility for the Portland congregation for a short period. Then he moved on, first to Seattle and then to San Francisco, to head Apostolic Faith Church congregations in those cities. During the time the two leaders worked together, they reportedly had a fairly good, yet curious relationship. Interestingly, the two seldom spoke of each other in their correspondences, and the denomination's historical account never mentions Trotter's work.

One reason for this exclusion may be that, at some point after 1913, Trotter became one of the early Pentecostal leaders to move into the oneness camp. Since Crawford opposed this movement, and was an outspoken critic of its leaders and did not fellowship with those with whom she disagreed, she naturally severed relations with Trotter.[32]

Over time, Crawford's most trusted ministry ally and confidant came to be her son, Raymond. At the time Florence went to Azusa Street, Raymond was a young man of sixteen. Even then, he was heavily involved in her ministry. Yet, after she moved to Portland, Ray wrote to his mother that he was going to join the navy. She did not answer his letter, but "prayed until the sun rose the next morning."[33] Subsequently, he had a change of heart, deciding to join her in Portland. Two years later, he was ordained at the age of nineteen. For the next twenty years, he served as his mother's assistant overseer. After her death, he succeeded her as general overseer, a position he held for nearly thirty years until his death in 1965.

Raymond spearheaded much of the Apostolic Faith Church's evangelistic ministry. Along with taking several transcontinental evangelistic tours by car, he piloted the airplanes used in aerial evangelism. And, despite his initial reluctance to join his mother in Portland, the two collaborated over several ministry efforts that were to have lasting effects on the denomination. Even though Florence and Raymond enjoyed a close relationship, Florence was reportedly heavy-handed in her dealing with most other people and her leadership style was extremely sectarian.

Her followers picked up from Raymond the habit of calling Crawford "Mother"—not pastor, bishop, or reverend—and found in her stern, yet nurturing, demeanor a matriarch who watched over her church family with protective zeal, but allowed no deviation from the standard she set. Crawford sought to maintain "unity" by squashing any hint of dissention that might arise. If she sensed discontent or a problem brewing, she would call a "saints meeting" to expose it and restore her authority-openly rebuking, disciplining, or dismissing the responsible party without allowing that person the opportunity to be heard by a deliberative body. A participant in one of these early meetings recounts:

> I'll never forget how the meeting affected us and how we reacted. We were all eager for God to have his full way in our lives and were eager to do his will and have his Spirit in our midst. We needed teaching and mother gave it to us. As she talked, different ones in the group spoke up and asked forgiveness of someone else present. This had an effect on the spirit of all who were there. The work then went forward with more power. The presence of God's Spirit was more powerful in the meetings, and more souls were saved than ever before.[34]

Despite the strong loyalty Crawford enjoyed from most members of her organization, her work was not without outside detractors and her leadership did not go completely unchallenged. Of course, she encountered the usual antagonism from male colleagues.

The rigid requirement that all pastors come to Portland each summer for the three-month camp meeting was another area of contention. During these sessions, Crawford held court, preaching on some aspect of her "Latter Rain Gospel" and expounding on the doctrines of the Apostolic Faith Mission. She saw this as a time to train pastors for more effective ministry. But many pastors saw it as a hardship on their fledgling congregations, which were left to fend for themselves in their pastors' absences.

In 1919, twelve years after establishing her first congregation, the undercurrent of discontent gave way to full-fledged confrontation with Crawford. A group of male evangelists and pastors led by Fred Hornshuh, a pastor from Eugene, Oregon, attempted to have a hearing with Crawford over these issues, but was refused. He, along with F. E. Crook, a minister from Dallas, Oregon, dissolved their relationship with the Apostolic Faith Mission. With their wives and eight other ministers, they formed the Bible Standard Mission. The split may have ostensibly resulted from Crawford's heavy-handed management, but many of the male pastors who had served under her were also uncomfortable with or resented what they saw as female domination of the organization. This disdain for women's leadership had unfortunate fallout from the very beginning of the Bible Standard Mission. At its first conference the leaders decided that "women could preach, but not lead."[35]

Crawford died in 1936 at age sixty-four. By the time of her death, the Apostolic Faith Mission had grown to only nine churches within the geographical bounds of the United States. Since her death, the growth of the Apostolic Faith Church has remained relatively small, especially in the United States, where, by 2006, there were forty- eight congregations. Its greatest presence is its international constituency, since missions have always been a focal point for its ministry. Crawford held camp meetings in Canada as early as 1907, and missionaries were in Scandinavia in 1911. Even so, it was not until 1943 that the first Apostolic Faith Church congregation outside the United States was established, in Roddickton, Newfoundland. Before that time, the denomination had primarily spread its message through an aggressive literature campaign.

The denomination's current periodical, Higher Way, is published in fifteen languages and sent to two hundred countries.[36] It currently has a circulation nearing one million copies. Additionally the organization produces Christian literature, including tracts, sermon notes, hymnals, and Sunday school materials in seventy-two languages. Much of these are available free of charge upon request.

During Crawford's lifetime, the bulk of her personal ministry remained centered around the city of Portland. With the financial and spiritual support of a strong congregation that grew to several hundred, she sent the Latter Rain Gospel from Portland to large cities and small towns around the country and the world. Today there are nine congregations in Canada, six in Romania, several hundred in Africa (six hundred alone in Nigeria, where the first church was not started until 1966), two in Australia, nineteen in Asia, ten in Europe, and fifteen in the Caribbean.

Women's Ministry and Leadership

While developing a clear picture of the life and ministry of the elusive Florence Crawford is difficult, establishing a realistic portrait of the ministry and leadership of women in the local Apostolic Faith Mission and Apostolic Faith Church that developed out of it is even more so. The resources for determining what role women were allowed to play are scattered in bits and pieces throughout a small number of

Crawford's sermons on the subject and some anecdotal evidence that surfaces throughout the denomination's historical narrative.

A first, cursory look at information produced by the Apostolic Faith Church might lead one to believe that Crawford was the only woman to hold a position of any substantial significance within the organization. One might be tempted to assume that Crawford was biased against working with other women or involving them in leadership. Certainly, information is available about several men who served in Crawford's organization. Despite the reticence of the Apostolic Faith to call attention to individual accomplishments, within the historical accounts several men are, at least briefly, identified and given credit for specific contributions to the denomination. For example, besides Will Trotter, who served faithfully at Crawford's side for a decade, and Raymond, who succeeded his mother as general overseer, Loyce Carver served in positions of increasing authority, then succeeded Raymond as general overseer.

From the Apostolic Faith Mission's early years, no other woman has ever risen to the highest ranks of leadership. Clara Lum, Crawford's trusted Azusa Street colleague, held vital responsibilities in the early organization, but most women have served in supportive roles. Crawford made few public pronouncements regarding women's ministry and leadership, and most of the denomination's statements do not refer to the issue, though she and her group were not completely silent on the topic. A number of strongly-worded sermons spelled out her position regarding women's roles in the home as well as the church. Her position, like Crawford herself, was not without contradiction. For her, women had spiritual freedom to be involved in ministry at every level of the church, yet had to be under subjection to their husbands in the home. She was clear that women were equally as called and spiritually suited for ministry as their male colleagues. Vivian Deno characterizes Crawford's position this way: "As other Pentecostals

59

urged women to return home and submit themselves to the authority of their husband and pastor, she refused to relinquish her spiritual autonomy or to defer to the authority of men, be they her pastor, local magistrates, fellow Pentecostals, or even her husband. Strong-willed and fiercely independent, Crawford in many ways challenges our understanding of Pentecostal.. women."[37]

Perhaps her most explicit statement of the role of women in the ministry was published in volume 18 of the Portland issue of The Apostolic Faith. In it, Crawford wrote a brief article entitled "Does God Call Women to Preach the Gospel as Well as Men?" In it she said,

> The Holy Ghost prophesies or preaches through one as well as another. In the days of the prophets there were five women that prophesied through the Spirit: Deborah, Huldah, Miriam, Noadiah, and Anna. When God could not get a man to lead Israel, He chose Deborah. And he is doing the same in the Holy Ghost dispensation....
>
> God promises twice to pour out His Spirit upon the women, and He has confirmed His promises by pouring out the Holy Ghost upon them in both the early and the latter rain. In this later outpouring of the Spirit, God has baptized about as many women as men and used as many women in preaching the Word, just as powerfully as the men and often more so...
>
> It is contrary to the Spirit of the Word to say that the Holy Ghost cannot preach and teach through a woman. In I Tim. 2:12, where many believe that women are forbidden to preach, we find that Paul is speaking of the family life

and of how a man should be the head of the house. He is not there speaking of the order in assemblies. Man is the rightful head of the family and the woman is not to usurp authority over her husband in the government of the home. Some claim that a woman should not speak in public assembly. But where Paul says the women should keep silence, he is speaking of disorder in the meeting, such as babbling and asking questions... [a]nd we forbid that today in the church of God. But this does not refer to witnessing or prophesying in the Holy Ghost. The Holy Ghost makes everyone a witness.[38]

In 1932, four years before Crawford's death, the Apostolic Faith Ministry issued a tract entitled "Women Preachers." The short, four-page treatise definitively affirmed the ministry of women and contended that much of the misunderstanding of the role of women was due to faulty exegesis of the two main Pauline restrictions found in scripture. It insisted that God "select[ed] women as well as men to fill offices among His people both under the Law and under grace" and that God "[m]akes no distinction between men and women; His gifts and callings are bestowed on each alike He bestows the prophetic or ministerial gifts upon his handmaidens as well as upon his manservants."[39] The pamphlet, which bears no attribution as to authorship, attacks the commonly held interpretation of the passage in Corinthians that directs silence for women in the church and the I Timothy passage forbidding a woman to teach. It contends that these passages cannot stand on their own merit, but must be understood within the context of a larger biblical picture of women receiving God's call to service.

61

The tract lifts several examples within scripture-Miriam, Huldah, and Deborah in the Hebrew Scripture, as well as New Testament references to Anna, the women at Jesus' tomb, the four daughters of Philip, and Priscilla. It notes the gender inclusiveness of Peter's speech on the day of Pentecost. Further, the author(s) insist that a deliberate distinction must be made between those women who are called of God and those who simply "usurp" authority. They further contend that the Apostle Paul would have been quick to "recognize and accept one who was called to the ministry, whether man or woman. Finally, they state, "We may therefore conclude from the Scriptures that the Word of God does not discriminate between men and women in respect to the gifts and callings of God."[40]

Within the Apostolic Faith Mission, women, as well as men, were called to various levels of ministry responsibility- though presumably, except for Crawford, the highest ranks were reserved for men. Women traveled, preached, taught, sang, and engaged in prison and harbor ministry alongside their male colleagues. What was important for Crawford and her followers was the sense that God had singled out an individual and anointed and gifted that person. And each person— male or female—had a responsibility to answer that call by making a tangible contribution to the ongoing ministry of the Apostolic Faith Church. The sheer variety and volume of ministry—conducting street meetings; automobile, harbor, and aerial evangelism; publishing and mailing; musical venues including soloist, ensembles, choir, and orchestra; missionary endeavors and support—required an army of unnamed workers, both men and women, who contributed their natural skills and spiritual giftedness.

Currently, though the majority of Apostolic Faith senior pastors are men, women serve as senior pastors and in other capacities of ministry within the organization. Three congregations, including those in Washington, DC, and St. Louis, Missouri, have women serving as senior pastors. Women cofounded churches in both Dallas, Oregon, and Chicago. There is one female pastor among Canada's six churches. Another woman, Zenida Ruis, pastors a local church and serves as jurisdictional leader, overseeing eleven churches and their pastors, in the Philippines.

The two most likely women to have been positioned by Crawford to move into leadership roles—her natural and adopted daughters— are conspicuously absent from the leadership and the narratives. During the early years of Florence's ministry, Mildred could be found at her side, worshiping or working on some ministry project. When she was ten, she appeared in the official Azusa Street Mission ministry staff portrait. Some scholars believe that, even at this early age, Mildred served as part of the credentialing board. She was an active participant in revival services, had her own Pentecostal experience, and traveled extensively with her mother to evangelistic campaigns (while her older brother was left at home with his father). Mildred's musical gifts even as a young girl had been recognized by her mother. In one account, Florence records her delight in her daughter's musical ability and the spiritual import she attached to it:

> Mildred composed a piece of music and sat down to play it yesterday. It took my soul almost out of this land, while she played it, and the power came on Sister Reece and she began to sing words, O so sweet and in such harmony with the music. How God flooded our souls as she sang. She could not remember them, but yesterday afternoon the power came on her again and she wrote them down. O you could hardly stay here, when they sing and play that piece. It's from the Paradise of God. If nothing else had happened but this, it ought to convince people.[41]

Yet, despite Crawford's contention in court that "God had commanded little Mildred to preach the doctrines of the Pentecostal faith,"[42] as Crawford's organization took shape and grew, Mildred sat on the sidelines. Her relationship with her mother, and with the church, was on and off and little is reported about her after those early years. There is evidence that for some period of her adult life she remained at least peripherally active in the church that her mother founded. It is known, for example, that Mildred was a soloist from time to time and collaborated with Raymond in writing several hymns that appear in the denomination's hymnal.

At one point she left the church and Portland altogether. She returned to the church in the early 1940s—after her mother's death—accompanied by her husband, Basil Robinson, and their children and served as a church soloist for a short time. Ultimately, however, she left the church again and severed all relationships with the organization for a period. Reportedly, during that period, she also separated from her husband and moved to Illinois, where she died around 1980.[43] Less is known about Crawford's adopted daughter, Virginia, who played an even more limited role in the local church or organization. Apparently, as an adult, she married and left the denomination altogether[44]

Legacy For Women

Crawford's contributions to the legacy of women's leadership at first appear insignificant. For many Christian women—even Pentecostal women clergy—the names Florence Crawford and Apostolic Faith Church mean little. Those outside the movement know even less of her. Further, because of the eccentricities of her organization, an initial investigation of her contribution to women's leadership within the broader Pentecostal realm might be expected to yield little fruit.

In an era of megachurches and church growth theory where the bottom line dictates that bigger is better, her impact in the American context is further limited by the relatively small number of Apostolic Faith congregations in the United States. Crawford's lifetime accomplishments seem minuscule. At her death, after thirty years of intensive evangelistic ministry, there were fewer than fifty Apostolic Faith Church congregations in the United States. Yet Crawford's criteria for success had little to do with numerical growth of the denomination she led. Instead, she was concerned with winning as many souls to faith in Christ as possible. Whether these souls became members of the Apostolic Faith Church was not important. Second, she was concerned with upholding what she saw as the biblical standard of holiness while protecting the Pentecostal movement from heretical teachings that compromised this standard. Indeed, those who. could not, or would not, live up to the rigid standard of piety she demanded were discouraged from affiliating with the Apostolic Faith Church.

Crawford was only peripherally concerned about the ministry of women and actually seemed to contradict herself on the issue. In her estimation, women were free to respond to whatever God called them to. At the same time, she insisted they were bound by scripture to maintain a posture of the submitted, supportive wife to the male head of the household. In essence, they were free to pursue their spiritual goals as long as that pursuit did not upset the home and call for neglect of their rightful places.

In her estimation, there was no distinction in ministry roles men and women could assume. Her few sermons on the topic communicate a strong spiritual egalitarian ethos. She continually asserted that God could call either men or women to any level of leadership within the church, and that the Holy Spirit could freely bestow ministry gifts on anyone. Further, she insisted that the man or woman on whom the

Spirit bestowed such gifts should not be held back by a spouse from fully pursuing ministry to which that person was called and for which he or she was gifted. This spiritual freedom stretched to cover a woman's choice in such practical spiritual matters as where she would attend church or with what Christian tradition she would affiliate:

> "When your husband tells you that you can't worship God, and you can't go to a certain place to worship God, he has overstepped the bounds of the law of the United States No man has any right to tell his wife where she shall worship, or how she will worship."[45]

Yet Crawford generally upheld traditional ideas regarding women in the home, distinguishing between women's freedom in spiritual matters and their required submission to their husband's authority in family matters. Though adamant about women's spiritual autonomy, she was equally adamant about the husband's authority in all temporal matters. In the same sermon, she insisted, "Aside from her religious rights, the husband] is the head of the household."

In line with traditional conceptions of women's role, Crawford contended that, although he may be neglectful, irresponsible, or even abusive, the husband and father was to be accorded this authority, Deno asserts that "Crawford's unflinching loyalty to the male-headed home limited the demands she made for greater social equality [for women]."[46] Crawford cautioned Pentecostal women to make their homes comfortable for their families and advised them that,

> [w]e are not to be running around from house to house as busy-bodies, but every woman should stay at home and keep her house clean and neat, because cleanliness is next to godliness. People claim to be godly and when you go into their

dirty kitchens, it will almost make you sick. Children are dirty, the mother has time to go to the neighbor and spend an hour when she should be cleaning up her house and her children. You are a million miles from the Bride of Christ if you do that.[47]

Crawford's stand on the husband's place in the home was coupled with the Apostolic Faith Church's priority on healing of breaches within families and the emphasis on the redemption of what they considered wayward husbands and fathers. A major concern of the church was reaching men who through drunkenness, revelry, reckless spending, and general dereliction of family responsibilities had caused their families to be without a head. The church sought to bring them to faith and bring about reconciliation with their initial spouse and families, even when this meant dissolving the family they were currently with.

This desire to restore fallen husbands to their rightful place was driven by an equally strong emphasis in Crawford's theology on the need for those who came to salvation to provide restitution for wrongs they had previously committed. This understanding had practical, and sometimes drastic, out-workings. If someone had stolen anything, that person was required to seek out the injured party and return the stolen goods. If someone had lied, the truth had to be told. But this emphasis on restitution also extended to those who through sinful action had injured or destroyed their families; they were to attempt to restore broken familial relationships. Parents and children were expected to apologize for past injuries. Those who had fractured their families either through desertion or divorce were to attempt to restore former relationships.

Earlier narratives of Crawford's marriage assumed that she, while taking her role as mother seriously and taking a rigid stand on these matters for others, failed to live up to this standard. They portrayed her as eschewing the traditional role of a wife and deserting her husband for a more active role in ministry. Conversely, Crawford was convinced that anyone, including herself, who had a living first spouse and had remarried was bound by God to sever the second relationship and attempt to restore the first marriage. For Crawford, however, an attempt to restore the first marriage was not possible. Her first husband had already remarried and was not interested in such a restoration. Her conviction that a second marriage while a first spouse was alive was adulterous was as strong as, if not stronger than, her conviction that a woman was to play a supportive role to her husband in the household. And ultimately this conviction, not her zeal for ministry, resulted in the dissolution of her marriage to Frank.

Conclusion

Even with these radical ideas regarding restoring broken families, Crawford exhibited a lived, practical feminism rather than an articulated feminism. While not often speaking or writing about women's rights, she was clear that, as a Spirit-filled woman, she had the same rights and responsibilities as her male colleagues to preach the Word of God. More importantly, she did not hesitate to take the reins of leadership from a male colleague when she felt more capable.

Yet Crawford's legacy to women is notable in a number of ways. First, her authoritarian leadership style closely resembles that of many male leaders. Such a style is not particularly viable for women's more communal leadership style. Many women deliberately try to avoid it and few can effectively appropriate such a model for their advancement. And although Crawford was surrounded by several capable women staffers, within her style there was little room for collegiality and even less room for mentoring a cadre of women to step into her shoes.

Crawford declined to engage the larger culture in a way that would allow her achievements to serve as a model for other women. During her lifetime, she and her organization maintained a separatist stance that ensured her voice was not heard in the ongoing conversations among Pentecostal leaders regarding this and other issues. This meant that Holiness-Pentecostal women saw a movement largely led by men, and many concluded that this must have been the way God intended it to be. Indeed, for a number of reasons, for most of the seventy years since her death, Crawford has remained an obscure figure, even within Pentecostalism. For women who looked for role models in the movement's history to help guide their actions, her story was unknown.

Crawford's practical feminism was complicated by her need to hold other convictions in balance. She failed to put forth a cohesive, theological foundation for the leadership of women, in part because the issue of women's place was only incidental to her more urgent focus on three other themes: evangelism, the need to make restitution and restore broken families, and the need to maintain a standard of holiness. Crawford failed to actively nurture other women to take on leadership positions. She was unable or unwilling to bring the two women closest to her—daughters, Mildred and Virginia—along. As they became adults, their relationship with her became more tenuous. Apparently, with the exception of Clara Lum, few women were counted among her close colleagues. Still, her unfolding story of achievements provides an additional resource for Pentecostal clergy women who attempt to navigate a place for themselves within the church's essentially male leadership.

As a strong, inner-directed woman, Florence Crawford was unafraid to do what she felt compelled do. As a woman of strong convictions, she articulated them with passion, convincing others of their value, and following them even to her own discomfort. She was less concerned with leaving a legacy for later generations than with

69

enlisting women and men to prepare her generation for Jesus' imminent return.

Mary Magdalena Lewis Tate
Church of the Living God, The Pillar and Ground of the Truth

Mary Magdalena Lewis Tate holds the distinction of being the first woman to receive the rank of bishop in a nationally recognized religious body: Thus, she holds the distinction of being the first woman to hold the rank of presiding bishop or head of a Protestant Christian denomination.[1]

Early Life And Ministry

Mary Street was born January 5, 1871, in Dickson, Tennessee, a small, rural community approximately forty-two miles southwest of Nashville.[2] She was one of four daughters[3] of John and Mary Street and reportedly was raised in a black family that was comparatively well-to-do for that time and place. Some sources indicate that Tate attended Tennessee Normal Institute Other sources contend that she had very little education, perhaps never attending public school, but instead was taught to read by her mother.[4] Regardless of her educational attainment, the constant boast of her followers was that Tate was a woman of obviously high intelligence and that the Bible was all she ever read and the only source she used or needed for her preaching and teaching.[5]

Tate was married three times. Her first marriage was to David Lewis, before 1890. From this union, Tate had two sons—Walter Curtis Lewis, born in 1890 probably near Vanlier, Tennessee, and Felix Early Lewis, born in 1892 in the same town.[6] This marriage ended in divorce in 1903 about the time that her ministry began. Lewis objected to his wife's street ministry. He accused her of desertion because of the amount of time she devoted to her newfound vocation and spent away from her family. Later, the two were to become good friends, and

Lewis and his new family became involved in his ex-wife's church and remained active in it until his death.[7]

As Tate's sons grew into young men, they often accompanied their mother on her preaching campaigns through the South and Midwest. When she could not afford to carry them with her, she left them in the care of various family members or close associates for short periods. Both boys professed Christian faith at young ages. As young men, both were to become actively involved in the leadership of Tate's ministry, contributing both spiritually and materially to their mother's vision.[8]

During his short lifetime, the older son, Walter, served as Tate's manager of affairs. In 1906, Tate ordained him bishop at the age of sixteen, and he was instrumental in establishing churches in Alabama, Georgia, New Jersey, Philadelphia, and parts of New England.[9] He also pastored the church in Chattanooga, Tennessee, where he lived. Walter died prematurely of pneumonia at age thirty-one in Chattanooga in 1921.[10]

Tate ordained her younger son, Felix, a bishop in 1914, at the age of twenty-two, in Quitman, Georgia. He served as one of the first state bishops" appointed by Tate and helped his mother establish the General Headquarters for the church in 1914.[11] He also established the New and Living Way Publishing House in 1923 and worked with his mother to compose and edit much of the church's early literature.[12] At Tate's death, Felix was ordained one of the three Dominion Chief Overseers and served in that capacity until his death in 1968 at age seventy-six.

Lewis' second husband, Elijah Estes,[13] was a part of the Church of the Living God at one time.[14] Little is known about that relationship, which also ended in divorce. Several years later, Estes was accused of adultery in an article published by Tate's son Felix.[15]

Mary Magdalena Lewis Estes married Elder Robert Tate in 1914 at age forty-three. Except that he was a minister, little is known about him or the circumstances of the marriage. However, Tate was reportedly responsible for the conversion of twelve members of her husband's family following the marriage.[16] Robert, however, does not appear to have played an active role in the leadership of the denomination.

Not much is known of Tate's early religious training or affiliation, though her first husband was reported to be a Methodist and she had been part of a Methodist congregation in her early years. She left that denomination due, in part, to her disagreement with some of the practices of the church as well as the church's stand against women being allowed to preach.[17]

Sometime after 1890, around the age of nineteen, Tate had a conversion experience and subsequently felt a call to preach. Some scholars insist that at some time during this period Tate was affiliated with William Christian's group, Church of the Living God (Christian Workers for Fellowship). Tate was later to insist that the major elements of her doctrinal stance came to her directly from God, but many of these elements, including the name itself and the exclusive use of water and unleavened bread in communion instead of wine or juice, were found in Christian's organization, which was founded in Wrightsville, Arkansas, in 1889.[18] We actually know little about what transpired in the fourteen intervening years between her conversion and call and the time she began preaching in Steele Springs, Tennessee, in 1903.

At the beginning, Tate's ministry involved door-to-door evangelizing and holding street preaching meetings and home Bible studies in her local community. It quickly broadened so that from 1903 to 1908 Tate traveled throughout the Ohio Valley and the South on what her followers were later to term "missionary journeys," to such cities as Brooklyn, Illinois; Paducah, Kentucky; St. Louis, Missouri; Paris, Tennessee; and Montgomery, Alabama. In each place, she preached and taught the doctrine she called "true holiness" in street meetings, going from house to house, and in revival type meetings in borrowed church facilities. In each of these communities, she established "holiness bands," which she called "do-right bands."[19] At first she did not attempt to organize them into a body or bring them under her personal control.

Tate spent time in the home of her two sisters, Queen Esther Edwards and Dora O'Neal, teaching them her newly developed beliefs. They became her first converts and were instrumental in helping her establish her ministry. In the earliest years, they kept her sons while she traveled. Later, both assumed much more active roles, becoming her first members, then ministers, and even later, bishops in the denomination. Her two daughters-in-law-Mary Francis Lewis and Helen Middleton Lewis-were both ministers and later bishops. After Tate's death, both these women were to serve as chief overseers of two of the three dominions that resulted from the partitioning.[20] Several of her grandchildren as well as nieces and nephews were involved in the early years. Many of them continued to be actively involved in the various factions that make up her legacy. Several took on leadership roles, becoming ministers, elders, and bishops.[21']

In 1903, Tate established her first church, the Latter Day Saints of the Foundation of True Holiness and Sanctification, as an independent congregation. There is no evidence that she initially had intended to do any more than found that congregation.

Like many early Pentecostals, Tate had been part of the Holiness movement. Speaking in tongues as evidence of that Holy Spirit baptism was not part of her early message. Her ministry began one year after Parham's initial Pentecostal revival and three years before the Pentecostal outpouring that began at Azusa Street. Indeed, it is unclear whether Tate was familiar with the occurrences of Parham's ministry or the Azusa Street Mission and the Pentecostal revival that sprang from it.[22] Her followers insist that she was generally unaware of these movements and independently arrived at an understanding of the initial evidence of tongues.

Literature produced by the Church of the Living God the Pillar and Ground of the Truth leads one to believe that Tate was completely unaware of the import of the Azusa Street Revival. Instead, it characterizes the revival that resulted from Tate's preaching as "the first great Pentecostal revival" and further states that "it is clear that God had not moved upon religious leaders of their day to teach Holy Ghost Baptism..." and that "[s]he, herself, had never seen the manifestation of the power of God in such manner upon anyone except herself at that time."[23]

Tate's own experience of the baptism of the Holy Spirit and speaking in tongues resulted from a crisis episode. In 1908 (two years after the beginning of the Azusa Street Revival), Tate suffered a nearly fatal illness that left her temporarily paralyzed. Although not initially expected to survive, she was miraculously healed. At the same time, she experienced the baptism of the Holy Spirit with the evidence of speaking in tongues and began to embrace and preach Pentecostalism.[24] As she began to share the experience with her followers and associates, they originally thought that she was mentally ill. However, she was able to convince them of the reality of the experience and their need to be partakers of it. So the doctrine of the baptism of the Holy Spirit with initial evidence of tongues was added to her stance on the need for true holiness and sanctification.

Establishing the Church of the Living God

In 1908, Tate held a series of revival meetings in Greenville, Alabama, in which some one hundred people experienced the Holy Spirit baptism with tongues. This meeting was the catalyst for a new congregation, which ultimately became the nucleus for a

77

denomination— the Church of the Living God the Pillar and Ground of the Truth, a name Tate claimed God revealed to her, through her son, Felix, as the true name for "God's latter-day house."[25]

Later that year, Tate was ordained a bishop by the board of trustees of her organization. By that time, the increasing number of holiness bands[26] that had been formed under her leadership evolved into her first full-fledged congregations and the core of her new organization. With the forming of the denomination, she was named First Chief Overseer.[27] The denomination began to grow and church plantings increased in towns throughout the rural East Coast as one person after another moved into a new community, carrying the doctrine of "true holiness." They shared with family members, who first accepted this doctrine, and subsequently started meeting together with others in the community to promote Tate's doctrine along with the Pentecostal doctrine of the baptism of the Holy Spirit with tongues. Tate and other denominational leaders would then send a team—often a man and woman—to take over the leadership of the congregation and get the church on solid footing.

Using this evangelistic strategy, Tate's body grew to little more than one hundred congregations under her direct authority and no more than two hundred congregations in related schismatic denominations by the time of her death. Most of these congregations had constituencies of less than one hundred members. During her lifetime, the total constituency never grew to more than several thousand persons, most of whom had personally sat under Tate's ministry at one time or another. As her denomination grew, Tate traveled throughout the East Coast to speak to her constituents, encourage them in the faith, preach revivals, and fight schisms that would arise from time to time.

By 1910, Tate's organization had additional congregations in Georgia. In that year, however, the first schism occurred. Out of this

78

came the first distinct body to grow into a separate denomination-the First Born Church of the Living God, under the leadership of Henry Joseph Echols. At the time of the schism, Echols was pastoring a growing church and had been elevated to the rank of bishop.[28]

By 1914, Tate's organization had established congregations in Illinois, Alabama, Kentucky, Florida, and Tennessee. Additionally, it had appointed four state bishops and published the first Constitution, Government and General Decree Book, In that year, a second schism occurred when Bishop R. A. R. Johnson left to form the House of God, Holy Church of God, the Pillar and Ground of the Truth House of Prayer for All People (Hebrew Pentecostal). Part of the reason for this schism was doctrinal, yet the new body kept the holiness roots inherited from Tate while adding several Judaic concepts, including keeping the literal Saturday Sabbath and several of the Jewish festivals, especially Passover.[29]

By 1916, Tate's organization had spread to nineteen states, Washington, D.C., and several foreign countries.[30] In that year, a third schism occurred when Bishop Archibald White led his growing Philadelphia congregation into the House of God, the Church of the Living God, Pillar and Ground of the Truth, Inc. This schism, in particular, was partly over the issue of women's leadership. White, like Mason of the Church of God in Christ, was initially ordained in the Baptist Church, held a conservative position regarding women's leadership, and did not approve of women as bishops.[31] So, indeed, this new faction somewhat restricted women's roles. The fact that each of the three schisms was orchestrated by male leaders may indicate that, though it existed, women's leadership was far from fully accepted and not without challenge even in a milieu where least expected-an organization founded by a woman. These men had risen in the ranks of Tate's organization, from minister to elder, then to bishop, and each had some level of corporate responsibility. Yet, each left to establish his own body. Though only one split ostensibly occurred over the issue of gender, none of the resultant organizations made the same place for women's leadership as did Tate's.

In 1923, Felix Lewis worked with his mother to open the New and Living Way Publishing House and Bookstore in Nashville, Tennessee. This city had become the organization's headquarters and Tate's home. From 1923 to 1940, the Publishing House supplied the church with Sunday school literature, music resources, and at least two periodicals—Another Comforter and The Official Organ-as well as other printed material. The periodicals recorded notices of and reports from special meetings, and testimonies of healing and other blessings from various members of the scattered congregations. Primarily, however, these periodicals were doctrinal in nature and did not focus specific attention on Tate and her activities.

Besides contributions to in-house publications, Tate apparently wrote little. There is little evidence that she showed the same appreciation for the possibility of use of electronic or written media for evangelism or outreach purposes as did McPherson and Robinson. Perhaps she lacked the financial resources to benefit from this new technology, which had not reached the level of use that it achieved during McPherson's and Robinson's ministry twenty years later. At any rate, there is no record of her having been involved in extensive writing (beyond the doctrinal literature and pastoral letters) or in broadcasting.

One medium that she used was music, specifically hymnody. As a prolific songwriter, her written legacy consists primarily of a hymns sung in her church during her lifetime and collected in a compilation titled *Spiritual Songs and Hymns*. This denominational hymnal was published posthumously in the late 1930s by Tate's daughter-in-law, confidante, and successor, Mary Frances Lewis Keith.[32] These works provide some of the most direct clues to Tate's theology, including some indication of her views of women's ministry and leadership.

Many of Tate's hymns allude to the mothering aspects of womanhood. Indeed, Jon Michael Spencer, noted African American musicologist, contends that the hymns of Tate's church "affirmed womanhood and the religious freedom of women," and "[n]o other hymnal of any Protestant denomination has ever affirmed womanhood in this way."[33]

Also prominent among her hymn themes are eschatological and soteriological ideas. Because Keith failed to document authorship of individual works within the volume, however, it is not possible to determine definitively how many or exactly which hymns were authored by Tate. Excerpts from one hymn definitely attributed to her,[34] give evidence of the vivid imagery and strong soteriology of her hymnody. It mixes Old and New Testament metaphors to paint a negative picture of one woman and reveal a strong sense of retributive justice:

Listen to a story about Jezebel,
Her sins were wicked, Jezebel got angry,
Her soul went leaping and jumping down in hell.
Way back yonder in olden days,
John told Jezebel about her ways.
Your evil deeds have ruined the land,
Repent, 'cause the Kingdom of God is at hand.
She got mad at John because he told her about the gospel.
She told her servants to boil him in oil.

In the refrain of the hymn, Tate sternly echoes this theme:

Jezebel, Jezebel, oh Jezebel
God done got tired of your wicked ways
The angels in the heaven numbered your days

81

Because of your evil ways,
God done got tired
You got to go to judgment to stand your trial.[35]

Outside of hymns, Tate confined her writing to denominational material.[36] Direct evidence of her theology is limited to such sources as the *Constitution, Government and General Decree Book,* first written in 1915 and revised in 1924. This book portrays Trinitarian movement, embracing Wesleyan holiness doctrines while critiquing its Methodist foundations.[37]

Though Tate saw herself as primarily called to revive the New Testament church, there is evidence that her vision went beyond purely spiritual concerns to include an interest in developing the social and educational needs of her followers. Specifically, Tate had a vision for developing "institutions and... educational facilities for the Church, Bible training schools and business colleges, general and local orphanages and rescue homes, academies, local schools and... facilities along educational lines necessary for the church"[38]

Tate took steps to make her social vision a reality. She set up guidelines for establishing, administering, and financially supporting the institutions.[39] For several years, while Tate resided in Orlando Florida, for example, she established and ran an elementary school using funds from the general church. Two offerings a year were set apart to support the educational work, including the elementary school, as well as a proposed Saint Mary Magdalene College and other schools and colleges throughout the country.[40] These other institutions never materialized. The various iterations of the Church of the Living God practice the episcopal form of government put into place at its inception. They generally have a board of bishops, a board of elders, and a general assembly for conducting church business. But, in actuality, during Tate's lifetime, she held an extraordinary degree of

82

power within the organization and most actual decision-making rested within her hands. She had, for example, "complete authority to approve, disapprove, and annul any rule or decree made by any person... in... or out of the Church if such rule or decree [wa]s intended for the Church of the Living God, the Pillar and Ground of the Truth."[41] Additionally, the Chief Overseer's name was to appear on "each and every" deed entered into by local congregations.[42]

In 1930, Tate contracted frostbite in her feet while conducting a winter preaching tour in Philadelphia. She died in that city on December 28, 1930, at the age of fifty-nine, from complications of diabetes and gangrene. She was buried in the family plot in Dickson, Tennessee. In 1963, her remains were relocated to Nashville's historic Greenwood Cemetery and a marker was erected memorializing Mother Tate near the cemetery's entrance.

Before her death, the founder established procedures for an orderly succession. *The Constitution, Government and General Decree Book the Church of the Living God* had specific instructions calling for an Executive Council of Bishops and Elders to seek God's will concerning who should be installed as Chief Overseer upon Tate's death. Though this procedure was faithfully followed, no consensus could be reached regarding a single successor[43] Instead, the council initiated a "temporary" arrangement in which three people who had worked closely with Tate during her lifetime were selected to run the organization. The office of Chief Overseer of the Church of the Living God was divided into three geographical regions (dominions); each of the three persons was given responsibility for overseeing one of the respective regions, each of which encompassed sixteen of the then forty-eight states.[44]

Once the arrangement was in place, however, repeated attempts to resolve the stalemate proved fruitless and a permanent three-way separation occurred. Each body pays allegiance to the legacy of work

83

and doctrine of Tate. Each retains some part of the original title of the founding body. Each dominion has its own independent governing structure and headquarters. Over the ensuing years, the respective dominions have been involved, from time to time, in litigation among themselves concerning the disposition of assets of the mother church.[45]

A Unique Doctrine

Tate's organization must be categorized as Holiness-Pentecostal in doctrine and practice. It shares with this movement belief in the baptism of the Holy Spirit with evidence of tongues. With the broader Evangelical community, it shares the assertion of the authority of scripture as the inspired Word of God. In addition, the denomination describes itself as sharing basic beliefs with other Christian bodies.[46] Yet Tate's primitive scriptural exegesis, without benefit of other resources, led to a distinctive understanding of Christian faith that stood her against her contemporaries even within the Pentecostal movement. With this primitive exegesis (which Tate called direct revelation by the Holy Spirit), she introduced several elements that she claimed were uniquely revealed to her as reviver of the true New Testament church. Following her teaching, the resultant organizations maintain several core beliefs that placed her at odds with other Christian denominations.

First, Tate insisted that the name of her organization was divinely unique, and the only true God-given name for the church. Other contemporary churches, she insisted, assumed names not sanctioned by God. Tate taught that assuming such "nicknames" was "dangerous."[47] Obviously, her followers and even her later detractors took the point regarding the church's name as seriously as did Tate. Each faction that broke from the original body retained the phrase

84

"Church of the Living God" as part of its name. Most also retained "Pillar and Ground of the Truth."

Along with the special name, the perceived uniqueness of her calling and that of her organization is reflected in her followers' assessment of the special significance of Tate's ministry, even among the already special significance Pentecostals generally ascribed to themselves. Their belief that her endeavor was "the beginning of true holiness in the last days" is reflected in declarations such as this:

> The Church of the Living God, The Pillar and Ground of the Truth was established in these last days by Saint Mary Magdalena, who is also an apostle Elder of Jesus Christ, by the will of God and chiefly an Elder of the Church, a mother, a light to the nations of the earth. Saint Mary Magdalena, the First [Chief Overseer and true Mother in True holiness.[48]

The perceived uniqueness is further reflected in the titles by which Tate's followers address her. Titles such as "Reviver" and "Chief Overseer," "Senior Bishop" and "Apostle Elder" testify to their conviction that her movement is the revival of the New Testament church in a way that was different from every other existing movement or denomination. Though she was affectionately called "Mother Tate" by those who knew her, many official documents of the organization and its successors ascribe these more formal titles to her.[49]

Although Tate held to the Pentecostal understanding of communion as an ordinance rather than a sacrament, she and her followers used water, rather than grape juice or wine, and only unleavened bread. The exclusive use of water comes from the belief that water, not wine, is a part of Christ's blood that flowed from his pierced body on the cross.[50] It also comes from a strong prohibition against partaking of any kind of alcoholic products, including

85

medicines that contain alcohol. The restriction on leaven comes from the Old Testament Passover. In the Decree Book, communion is often referred to as Passover.[51] Another unique feature of communion within the Church of the Living God is the practice of always following it by foot washing, a symbolic ritual in which every member is expected to participate.

The denomination holds a Sabbath understanding of Sunday, declaring it a day of rest when members are expected to abstain from work and participate wholly in worship services. It appears that this belief is based on a misunderstanding of the relationship of the Hebrew Scripture's position on Saturday as Sabbath and the New Testament understating of Sunday as the Lord's Day. However, Tate based her position on a number of individual texts that she felt upheld her position, as outlined in the following hymn she authored:

Now listen unto me and understand what I say!
God is the very one who instituted the Sabbath Day.
Read Genesis 2 and 2. Now you know God's word is true,
    yes.
It's written in the law you see, and it's not too old for me,
It's just like not drinking wine. Acts 13 and 27, you will find.
Now you had better not work on Sunday, it's a sin and a
    shame.

Read Exodus 20th Chapter, beginning in the third verse.
Surely if you work on Sunday, it's the Sabbath, you will
    surely be cursed.
Read Hebrews 4 and 4, if you don't want to read no more,
Read Acts Chapter 16 and verse 13, tells how and where
    the Saints Convened to meet on the Sabbath day
To teach and hear what the word of God did say;

And they did not work on Sunday, it's a sin and it's a
    shame

The Spirit tells us in Titus, chapter 3, and one.
To be subject to principalities sand powers, so let God's
    will be done.
And be subject to magistrates, to be ready to every good
    work.
They all OK's Sunday for Sabbath. See Acts 13 and 14
    verse.
I regret I did not know the Sabbath all way from my birth.
Then I never would have worked on Sunday, it's a sin and
    it's a shame.

Monday, Tuesday, and Wednesday are half the working
    days we see,
So Thursday, Friday and Saturday, these make the other
    three;
And Sunday is the seventh day, it shall ever be Sabbath to
    me.
Read Exodus the Twentieth verse of chapter 23,
And you better not work on Sunday, it's a sin and it's a
    shame.[52]

Tate led the Church of the Living God with a rigid standard of
personal piety. Along with restrictions on alcoholic beverages,[53] her
standard prohibited eating pork, swearing or taking oaths, gambling,
dancing, or participating in or attending sports events, and attending
movies or reading fiction. Members were also expected to tithe.
Moreover, membership was limited to those who had received the
baptism of the Holy Spirit with evidence of tongues.[54] To maintain the

standard of "true holiness" within the body, fellowship with other churches was prohibited. Access to the pulpit was limited only to ministers who were members of the denomination.

Tate did not see her movement as simply another segment of the Holiness or Pentecostal movement. Rather, she saw it as an attempt to "reestablish" the New Testament church in such a way as to restore a purity and holiness far greater than in the restorationist thrust generally found in Pentecostalism. Tate felt that her Pentecostal brothers and sisters did not go far enough in restoring the church's purity and that God had uniquely revealed to her the name of the church, Sabbath rest, water for communion and regular washing of the saints' feet, and she felt these were essential elements of such a restoration. Tate and her followers saw themselves as filling a void in which the "light of holiness and sanctification was so obscure that the people who first heard her marveled at the pureness of the Word and hailed it as a new faith and doctrine."[55]

Some followers and others contend that Tate was influenced by the teachings of Mary Baker Eddy, founder of the Christian Science Church.[56] Others maintain, however, that any apparent influence of Eddy is purely coincidental, though there were some striking similarities.[57] Like Eddy, she sensed the appropriateness of women holding leadership roles in the church. In addition, Tate, like Eddy, saw her teachings as previously undisclosed revelation. Finally, like Eddy, Tate was especially attracted to a belief in divine healing to a degree that went beyond the emphasis that even other Pentecostals placed on the doctrine.[58]

Tate believed in praying for the sick, and several testimonies from members of her organization highlight the strength of that belief and importance attached to it. They recount "miraculous" healings that allegedly came about because of her prayers, even though she herself suffered from chronic diabetes. Tate hoped that her followers would diligently accept and practice her teachings on healing but sensed that many of them were not up to her level of faith in this area. On her death bed, she reportedly chided her followers, "If the saints had the same faith for me that I have had for them, I would be healed."[59]

Her emphasis on divine healing included foregoing the use of doctors and conventional medicine. To Tate, those Christians who had genuinely strong faith could live entirely without doctors and medicine. For her, only weaker Christians needed to resort to conventional methods. Many of her followers subscribed to these teachings and, according to their testimonies, lived relatively healthy lives. Interestingly, however, both she and her older son died prematurely from conditions that might have benefited from conventional medical care.

Women's Ministry and Leadership

Tate did not see her main purpose as either furthering the cause of women's ministry and leadership within the Church of the Living God, Pentecostalism, or the wider church. Instead, she saw herself as divinely and uniquely ordained by God to restore the church to true New Testament holiness. Since furthering the ministry and leadership of women was not her primary focus, Tate did not often speak publicly or write extensively about women's leadership. We must look, therefore, at her concrete actions regarding women's leadership and authority within the Church of the Living God to establish her stand and assess her contribution in this arena.

The question becomes, how were ideas of the equality of women actualized in practical ways within her denomination? How were women deployed in ways that facilitated their movement into positions of ministerial leadership? The answer is, at least in part, that Tate took substantial steps to ensure that women would assume important roles in the leadership of her body almost from its very inception.

During Tate's administration, women as well as men were ordained to every level of ministry-minister, elder, and bishop. Women were appointed to positions of authority, such as district and state overseers, in numbers equal to those of men. Women as well as men were placed as pastors into existing congregations. They were sent to plant new works and to nurture them to viability as congregations.

Men and women often went out in pairs to plant new congregations or to build up faltering congregations. Sometime after 1920, for example, Tate sent Malissie Kelly and her brother Moreland Williams (both later to become bishops) to Gainesville, Florida, to assist in establishing a congregation there. C. D. Braddy joined his mother-in-law, Sophie M. Jewell (who both also later became bishops) in Jacksonville. They built a successful congregation there, then moved on to places such as Cosmo, West Palm Beach, and Ocala, Florida, as well as cities in Georgia and New Jersey.[61] This pattern was repeated with varying degrees of success by different pairs. Sometimes the woman was the leader. Sometimes it was the man.

While Tate maintained a pattern of relative gender equality in deployment of ministers by her organization between 1908 and her death in 1931, and though she regularly deployed women as well as men to plant and help new churches grow,[62] nevertheless, in one of her first significant acts in organizing her churches into a denomination, she failed to seize the opportunity to underscore the ideal of women's equality in ministry. In 1914, when Tate and the General Assembly appointed the first four state bishops, all four appointees were male. These included her sons, Felix and Walter, and two others identified only as J. D. Pagitt and B. J. Scott.[63] Despite this singular act, however, the pattern of all male leadership beyond the congregational level did not persist. In a surviving statement addressing women's leadership in

90

the church, Tate was very clear that there should be no distinction based on gender and extended this understanding of equality to include racial equality in the church:

> God has already told us in his word that there are no distinctions made on sex regarding leading the church. His word states that there is neither male nor female, Jew nor Greek, bond nor free... but we are all one in Christ. If Christ can move the sex and race barrier, why can't we? In reality God does not see sex... he sees a spirit. All Christians receive the same Spirit. There is not a separate Spirit for men and women. A woman receives the same Spirit as a man, therefore she can do any work in the church that a man can.[64]

The relative absence of a significant body of public pronouncements regarding women's leadership must not overshadow Tate's own example of strong women's leadership. She acted purposefully and resolutely to accomplish what she saw as her God-given mission. She did not waver when confronted with hostilities; each attack and schism left her more determined to achieve her vision of establishing a pure holiness church. As she moved to do this, she unobtrusively incorporated a commitment to the equality of women in the ministry and leadership of the church.

As part of her strategy for reviving the church, Tate sought out and nurtured women as well as men whom she felt had particular ministry gifts to develop, placing them strategically tom contribute to the fledgling denomination. The men included Walter and Felix, along with Bruce McLeod, who later headed one of the three dominions.

Tate's influence on women's leadership was mitigated by the familial structure of her organization. Many of the women (and men) who rose to the most prominent positions were related to Tate by

91

blood or marriage, and sometimes by both—her sisters, her daughters-in-law, her granddaughters, her great granddaughters, and her nieces.

This structure provided a degree of control over the direction these organizations followed and ensured a degree of theological as well as personal loyalty to the founder. So, any proclaimed allegiance to open opportunity for leadership without regard to gender was diminished by this restriction of actual opportunity to the top leadership to a few, trusted family members. For example, Tate's daughters-in-law, Mary Frances Lewis and Helen M. Lewis, and Gladys Lewis Sherrod, the daughter of her son Felix, received special attention and nurturing, serving as her apprentices. And, indeed, all the women who eventually ascended to the position of Chief Overseer of one of the three dominions were, somehow, related to Tate.

Bishop Mary F. Lewis Keith, one of her closest confidants and colleagues and assistant pastor,[65] was ordained a bishop in 1923 and served as the organization's general secretary-treasurer. After Tate's death, Keith assumed the leadership of one of the three dominions. She continued Tate's legacy of social as well as spiritual leadership, opening the Keith Bible Institute to educate the leaders of her organization and the House of God Home for Children. Moreover, Keith posthumously edited and financed the publication of Spiritual Songs and Hymns, the hymnal that attributes many songs to Tate's possible authorship.

Helen Middleton Lewis, Tate's second daughter-in-law, lived in Tate's homes in Nashville and Dickson, Tennessee, and had a close relationship with the founder before marrying her son. She was called to the ministry in 1928, three years before Tate's death and the same year in which she married Felix. In 1932, one year after Tate's death, she was ordained a bishop within the Lewis Dominion.

Before Tate's death, Helen was instrumental in establishing several congregations. She had served as assistant pastor of the Crystal City,

92

Florida, congregation, pastor of the Daytona Beach congregation, and district elder of the West Coast district of Florida. After marrying Felix, she served as assistant Chief Overseer and general secretary-treasurer of the Lewis Dominion, effectively placing a major portion of the governing authority in the couple's hands.

Before assuming the position of Chief Overseer, Helen Lewis had served in a variety of positions. From 1931 to 1950, Helen served as pastor of the church in Nashville. In 1932, she was appointed district bishop of Kentucky and Indiana. When the family moved to West Palm Beach, she was appointed pastor of the church there and presiding bishop of a portion of the East Coast District of Florida.

Gladys Lewis Sherrod was a close confidante and companion of her grandmother and a leader in the church by age seventeen. At that early age, she was given the responsibility of serving as the main speaker for the Florida State convention. She was being groomed for further leadership, but she had married at an early age and died giving birth at age nineteen. At the time of her death, she had attained the rank of bishop.[66]

Yet, Tate did not limit her attention to the women directly related to her. She continuously identified, deployed, and promoted other women in planting congregations. Unlike other Pentecostal bodies, once the congregation matured, she often left these women in place or replaced them with other women.

The examples of Sophie Jewell, Malissie Kelly, and Mattie Lou McLeod are indicative of the lives of a number of women in Tate's organization. Sophie Jewell met Tate in Ocala, Florida, and invited her to teach a Bible study in her home that eventually led to the establishment of a church. Jewell was instrumental in helping to start other churches in Mt. Canaan and Jacksonville, Florida. She usually worked as one half of a partnership with her son-in-law, C. D. Braddy. They also were instrumental in building up churches in Georgia and

New Jersey. Both were eventually elevated to the rank of bishop. Along with planting and nurturing churches together, they shared joint appointments first as district bishops, then as state bishops.[67]

Malissie Kelly was instrumental in establishing several churches during Tate's lifetime. She served as pastor of the Gainesville, Florida church and donated land, and helped to build the church in St. Augustine, Florida. By the early 1940s, she was ordained a bishop by Felix Lewis. She later served as a district bishop over the area where she had pastored.[68]

Mattie Lou McLeod Jewell worked closely with Tate before her death. She was the wife of Bruce McLeod, who had worked alongside Tate's son, Felix, and who had assumed the oversight of one of the three dominions after Tate's death. Upon her husband's death, Mattie assumed the leadership of the McLeod Dominion. She, too, carried on Tate's legacy of social as well as spiritual leadership, establishing the Jewell Academy and Seminary that served grades kindergarten through high school and operated from 1950 to 1962.[69]

Legacy for Women

Each of the three factions resulting from the dissolution of Tate's denomination was headed by women at various times. However, Tate did not put steps in place to ensure that women would carry on the legacy of her denomination after her death. Moreover, the failure of her church to follow her wishes concerning passing on the denomination's leadership played a major part in the dividing of Tate's legacy.

For assessing her legacy, these three bodies are considered together for several reasons. First, each traces its origins directly back to Tate's original body. Second, each still exemplifies the theological characteristics of the mother body; the disagreement that resulted in the schism was primarily over political territory, not doctrine. Lastly,

94

each is tied to the original body by biology or marriage since Tate's leadership was disseminated principally to her heirs and it is among them that the schism occurred. For twenty-two years, from the founding of the Church of the Living God until Tate's death in 1930, there was a single body under Tate's headship. The earliest history, therefore, is shared by all three organizations, each of which dates its beginnings to the 1903 founding of Tate's first church.

A fourth group, The House of God the Church of the Living God, the Pillar and Ground of the Truth, Inc, which maintains its headquarters in Philadelphia and which might be called the White Dominion, broke away from the mother church more than a decade before Tate's death. Although publicly the reason for the split involved charges and counter-charges of adultery and the misuse of funds,[70] the issue of women's leadership was certainly, in part, also a key reason. White's conservative position concerning the leadership of women remained part of the fabric of his organization's structure as long as he was alive, for according to White's nephew, A. H. White's successor, his uncle "recognized the importance of women... [but] did not think too strongly of their roles as bishops especially if there were too many of them on the board of bishops, perceiving that they would cause too many problems."[71]

While the groups that broke off in 1910 and 1914 maintain a clear distance from Tate's group, as the largest of the bodies, White's group retained a similar name and still identifies itself as coming from the original organization. Although women in this group cannot achieve the rank of bishop, women may serve in jurisdictional leadership roles and on denominational boards—levels of leadership still higher than is found in some other Pentecostal bodies. Therefore, though historical continuity of the four bodies must be viewed as carrying the major portion of Tate's Pentecostal legacy, White's group was at least partially faithful in carrying out Tate's legacy of women's leadership.[72]

The McLeod Dominion became the Church of the Living God, the Pillar and Ground of the Truth Which He Purchased with His Own Blood, Inc., headed by Bishop Bruce L. McLeod. During the early years of Tate's tenure, McLeod was responsible for starting congregations in the Midwest and mid-South. He also helped Felix Lewis locate and purchase the property for the headquarters of Tate's denomination. McLeod headed his dominion from 1931 until his death in 1936. When he died, the leadership of the dominion fell to a woman—his wife, Bishop Mattie Lou McLeod,[73] who held the leadership for fifty-five years until her death in 1991. She moved the denomination's headquarters to Indianapolis, Indiana, and established Jewell's Academy and Seminary as well as a veteran's training program. In 1991, Jewell's granddaughter, Bishop Naomi Aquilla Manning, became the Fourth Overseer of the Church and served until her death in 2003.[74]

Felix Lewis headed the Lewis dominion, the Church of the Living God, the Pillar and Ground of the Truth, Inc., from 1931 until his death in 1968 Leadership then passed to Bishop Helen Lewis, who served as Chief Overseer pro tempore until the next year when she was officially selected Chief Overseer by the Supreme Executive Council Afterward, she worked with her son, Meharry Lewis, to reestablish the New and Living Way Publishing House and co-authored, with him, the church's doctrinal treatise, The Beauty of Holiness: A Small Catechism of the Holiness Faith in 1988. Helen served as bishop for thirty-three years until her death in 2001. At that time, her son assumed leadership.

Along with its distinct name, and the use of water instead of wine at communion, the Lewis Dominion identifies the biblical justification of women's equality in ministry as one of its three unique distinctives,[75] succinctly asserting in its doctrinal statement that, "God is no respecter of persons... and... summons women as well as men into the preaching and teaching ministry and other leadership positions of the church."[76] Further explication of that doctrine is provided in a longer statement, which, like most from the organization, attempts to provide a biblical foundation for the stance:

> Since gender and not ministry seems to have distinguished the prophets from the prophetesses of the Old Testament, it is reasonable to assume that both brought the Word of God to the people. Albeit, not all prophets or prophetesses were true [T]he Old Testament leaves us in no doubt that the ministry and title of "prophetess" was well established in the early house of God. A few examples are Deborah... Miriam... Huldah...

> The term preacher has been more closely associated with the ministers of the New Testament Gospels than with ministers of the Old Testament, yet the carrying of the Word of God was and is the work of both. In the Holiness faith, women as well as men have gender-unrestricted access to the pulpit and other offices of the church.[77]

In a 1988 article, in the Palm Beach [Florida] Post, then Chief Overseer Helen M. Lewis expounded on the denomination's stand on the ministry and leadership of women. Citing Galatians 3:28 as her foundation, she put it in this manner:

> We believe in women preachers, and we believe that women can hold any office in the church that a man holds. The Bible says there's neither Greek nor Jew, male nor female. But all are one in Christ Jesus... unwillingness to accept women preachers is responsible for so much of the diversity of churches today."[78] It is interesting to note, however, that in the same article, Lewis' endorsement of

women's leadership within the church still contains within it the traditional evangelical understanding of women's responsibilities in the home.

Paul's oft cited instruction to "let your women keep silence in the churches" was directed to "bossy" women... housework and raising children are a wife's job, not the husband's.

We believe that a woman should be subject to her husband... but the husband should not interfere if she feels a call to the ministry. We believe that the first right is to God, then the next right is to her husband and family.[79]

In essence, for Tate, women could move into any leadership role to which they were called, but this freedom did not release them from their responsibilities as wives and mothers. Neither was there any indication that the husband was expected to share in domestic responsibilities.

Tate's former daughter-in-law and confidante, Mary Lewis Keith, was elected to head the Keith Dominion, the House of God Which Is the Church of the Living God, the Pillar and Ground of the Truth without Controversy.[80] During the thirty-two years that Keith served, from 1931 until her death in 1962, this body has also upheld the legacy of the leadership of women. Following Keith's tenure, she was succeeded by Dr. James W. Jenkins, who served until 1990. The fourth, and current, Chief Overseer of the church is Bishop James C. Elliott.

The task of assessing Tate's legacy is made more difficult because of the disparity in statistics available from the six organizations that are heir to her ministry. By the time of her death, the strategies employed by Tate and her followers fostered a body of less than a hundred congregations under her direct authority. In all, no more than two hundred congregations existed in related schismatic denominations. Since most of these congregations had constituencies of less than one hundred members, during her lifetime, her total constituency grew to no more than several thousand persons.

Since her death, the bodies that are Tate's heirs have fluctuated in the number of churches and the size of membership. They have also been reluctant to share information on membership numbers. However, within the Lewis Dominion alone, as of 1988, there were some two thousand members.[81] The actual numbers of churches and members for the Keith Dominion and McLeod or Jewell Dominion (as it later came to be known) remain unreported. By the 1970s, the three branches had an estimated total combined constituency of more than five hundred congregations and approximately twenty thousand members.[82] When the schismatic Philadelphia branch, which reportedly has twenty-six thousand members in one hundred and ten churches,[83] and the two other schism bodies are included, the total rises to more than eight hundred congregations and at least fifty thousand members. Taken together, however, this would still constitute a relatively small denomination, even among Pentecostal bodies.

Despite her followers' assertions that Tate's life and ministry "influenced thousands around the world," she lived and ministered in virtual obscurity from all but a small band of committed supporters. The circumstances of her life, as a lower-class black woman, meant that she was almost completely ignored outside of her small circle, and that her immediate, tangible influence was restricted to a quilt-like patch of primarily rural communities scattered mainly along the East Coast of the United States. Even today, she remains largely obscure.

While newspapers across the country and around the world covered the events of the Azusa Street Revival, Tate's "revival" did not engage even the black press, which often sensationalizes most eccentric male cultic leaders. And, while scholars of every persuasion covered the most minute details of Aimee Semple McPherson's life and ministry, historians, biographers, and other scholars of American religion, in general, and of Pentecostalism, in particular, show scant interest in Tate, giving her little more than a footnote when providing already minimal coverage of the contribution of women.

The circumstances of race and class play some role in the lack of coverage of her life and ministry. Her constituency involved mainly poor, uneducated, predominantly (if not entirely) African Americans, in small towns with unfamiliar names such as Crystal River, Palatka, and Arlington, Florida, and Egg Harbor, New Jersey. Even while a small number of African American scholars of religion have acknowledged and celebrated the contributions of Tate's black sister, Ida Robinson, interest in Tate is just beginning to unfold and her story remains largely untold, even in the African American Pentecostal community.[84]

Tate showed little concern for secular issues not directly related to her perceived mission. Her concern was restoring the church to a high standard of personal piety, abstinence from social sins, and strict adherence to an Old Testament social and ritual ethic. She focused the majority of her time, energy, and resources in those areas but did almost nothing to ensure that even her spiritual contribution was preserved or disseminated to a broader public. As with most Pentecostal preachers of her day, she did not use a manuscript, but preached straight from her scripture text. Her sermons were not recorded and, apparently, no recorded sermons remain.

Tate followers boast that she" used no other resource but the Bible" to preach, teach, and develop doctrine. Her reluctance to draw from the rest of the Christian tradition is adversely reflected in the awkwardness of much of the writing that she did attempt. The few original materials that remain intact are replete with spelling

100

irregularities and awkward grammatical structures; they mix unrelated biblical passages to form what she saw as the foundational doctrines of true holiness.[85]

The impact of her influence was further limited because she did not avail herself of media to extend the reach of her ministry, as did Crawford, Robinson, and McPherson. Her writing did not go beyond directives for structuring and carrying out the organization's ministry and instructing constituents on practical aspects of living out of this vision of true holiness. Her doctrine and news of her ministry traveled primarily by word of mouth, largely through extended family networks, as members told their families and acquaintances of this charismatic woman who preached a unique doctrine and demonstrated the power of God in her ministry in a unique way.

Tate's development of doctrines on Sabbath-keeping, substitution of water for wine in communion, and the divine ordination of her organization's name left her group outside of the theological camp of "orthodox" or classical Pentecostalism. Mainline Protestant and even most Pentecostal bodies considered her views heretical. As a result, male church leaders (if they paid any attention at all) could point to her theology to bolster their argument against the leadership of women in the church. They identified her with other sectarian women leaders such as Ellen White, Rebecca Cox, and Mary Baker Eddy as indicative that women leaders are more prone to heresy than men because they are of weaker intellect and more open to deception. They could gloatingly point to elements such as Sabbath-keeping and substitution of water for communion wine and dismiss her and her organization as a heretical group led by one of those unstable women.[86]

Tate's potential influence on Pentecostal women's status was further limited because of her own separatist stance, which exaggerated the cultic tendencies of the group including such elements as the rigid personal piety and the restriction of membership to those who could personally testify to having actually experienced speaking in tongues. These were coupled with the insistence by Tate and her followers that this new doctrine that she alone preached was "true holiness." According to them, everything else was limited or tainted in some way. Further, fellowship with other churches was discouraged and access to the pulpit was limited to ministers who were members of the denomination. All this guaranteed that there was little opportunity for her vision of equality for women to gain a broad hearing within the wider Christian community-or even within mainstream or classical Pentecostalism.

Conclusion

Saint Mary Magdalena Lewis Tate is exemplary of a woman compelled to follow God's unique call to undertake the exceptional task of restoring the contemporary church to its New Testament purity. She did this without equivocation over whether women in general or she, specifically, could or should be involved in church leadership. Her response to this call set in motion the achievements that began with a young street preacher, going from door to door to tell her neighbors of a purer form of holiness, and ended with Tate in position as the first woman to preside as bishop over a nationally recognized denomination.

Though equality of women was not the primary focus of this vision, it was a principal of what Tate saw as the nature of a pure New Testament church. Her legacy includes several groups that continue to place importance on women's equality in church ministry and leadership. In spite of this significant achievement, her impact on Pentecostal women's leadership was limited by Tate's particular circumstances. The uniqueness of her doctrine, her deviation from orthodox Pentecostal theology, her separatist stance-even from other Pentecostals-and her failure to widely disseminate her message limited the impact of her legacy. Still, the Lewis Dominion stresses the importance of Tate's life and the scope of her accomplishments:

> Mary Lena Street was born... in the engulfing aftermath of American slavery with all of its attendant bruises and scars. She spent most of her early life in the rural South with little opportunity to obtain a formal education. These influences... were not unique... [but what is u]nique is the fact that this black woman would be endowed with an unquenchable determination to fulfill her destiny, not just "in the work" of the ministry, but as a fully capable and qualified preacher of God's Word. The unique combination of factors-a woman, black [and] untrained, the ministry, and the period (early 1900s)-even by today's standards... would strongly mitigate any powerful hope of realizing such an unlikely goal.

> The life of Mary Lena (Street, Lewis) Tate is significant because the plight and fight of women in their thrust to gain full status as productive and recognized citizens in all aspects of our world society is not yet a fait accompli. The accomplishment of this person is just one among many milestones which must be recognized as significant in the struggles of women.[87]

Tate modeled, as much as preached, a practical womanism that espoused equality of the sexes throughout the church. Even though her first four substantial appointees were male, she subsequently appointed and promoted women as well as men to every level of ministry. She deployed women to the same extent as men to promote true holiness, and rewarded those who served well with increasingly important responsibility and leadership roles, regardless of gender.

103

Women in these groups have enjoyed long tenures as denominational heads, but have not failed to share leadership with their male colleagues.

Equally as important, Tate modeled tireless leadership that was comparable to that of any male leader. She was involved in every aspect of the work of building and leading her young organization- preaching out new congregations, setting them in order, appointing pastors, adjudicating disputes within and between congregations, and developing doctrine and polity. In pursuing her vision, she sacrificed her marital relationships, a regular home life with her sons, and her health. Yet, she did not fail to carry out unwaveringly the heavy requirements that such a weighty vision forced on her. Her followers found in her a strength of character and conviction they continue to revere. Even today, she is still esteemed as "Saint Mary Magdalene."

Aimee Semple McPherson
International Church of the Foursquare Gospel

Considered by some the most widely recognized Pentecostal preacher of the early twentieth century, Aimee Semple McPherson was unmistakably the most colorful and controversial.. of the modern women apostles investigated. Vinson Synan, noted Pentecostal historian, has said of her that "[s]he holds a prominent rank among all religious leaders of the twentieth century, regardless of their sex, and may well be the most important ordained woman minister in the history of Christianity."[1]

This assessment might be an overstatement in a religious milieu in which many still regard Pentecostals as a sect populated by the marginalized. Yet flamboyance, antics, and reputation for controversy earned her the distinction of being the most well-known Pentecostal preacher of her time. According to one of her biographers, during the heyday of her ministry in the 1920s she made the front page of America's biggest newspapers at least three times a week on average.[2]

Amid the rigid personal asceticism that characterized early Holiness-Pentecostalism, when most adherents and leaders denounced stylish attire as "worldly" and most Pentecostal women could best be described as plain and unadorned, McPherson—petite, stylishly coiffed, and fashionably dressed- was physically attractive and striking in appearance[3] Some described her as looking more like a flapper than a Pentecostal preacher. At a time when most Pentecostals preached separation from "worldly" alliances, including those with the rich and powerful, her friends included politicians and movie stars as well as some of the most famous male preachers of her day within or outside the Pentecostal movement.

She could be found donning costumes of the angel Gabriel or a traffic cop to preach, or entering a worship service at Angelus Temple on a motorcycle and using the venue of dramatized sermons and operettas rather than rhetorical sermons to deliver the gospel. From an early age, she used her dramatic gift in school and church dramas and comedic presentations. Later, these same gifts were used to punctuate her sermons, hold the attention of thousands, and win many to a movement that "respectable" people often shunned. Her antics ensured that her face regularly graced the pages of America's largest newspapers and the most popular magazines during the 1920s, that she was listed as a tourist attraction in the guide to the southwestern United States throughout her lifetime,[4] and that several hundred books and articles have been written about her.

McPherson's reputation for controversy ensued first from the fact that within a very conservative, morally staid religious climate of early Pentecostalism, she had two failed marriages—one involving a clandestine elopement-and an alleged love affair with one of her employees. Second, she was involved in a mysterious disappearance that made the headlines of many newspapers and was the focus of several literary works.[5] Third, she was not averse to carrying the gospel message to arenas where other Pentecostal preachers would not go; she could be found preaching in makeshift tents, on Broadway stages, and in nightclubs. Further, she was continually embroiled in litigation with members of her family and staff. And, finally, after evidence of having earlier suffered at least one emotional breakdown, she succumbed to death from an "accidental" dose of sleeping pills just a few days short of her fifty-fourth birthday.

Early Life And Ministry

Aimee Kennedy was born near Ingersoll, Ontario, Canada, in 1890, the only child of James Kennedy, a devout Methodist, and his wife, Mildred, a Salvation Army member thirty years his junior.[6] Aimee was very religious as a young girl and actively participated in religious services in both denominations, gaining very different models of the role of women in church leadership. Her mother's Salvation Army heritage (with Catherine Booth as its female cofounder) openly affirmed the ministry of women as equals. Her father's Methodist tradition took a more traditional stand on women's leadership, allowing the few "exceptional" women to preach, while not explicitly supporting the equality of women.

After the usual period of adolescent religious doubting, she was converted in 1907, at the age of seventeen, at a Pentecostal revival meeting. She had first attended the meeting out of curiosity and initially found the worship experience, with its emotional exuberance, laughable. Very shortly, however, after sitting under the preaching of a young evangelist from Ireland, Robert Semple, Aimee felt a sense of conviction and had a conversion experience.

Aimee appears to have been a fairly good and popular student. Yet, shortly after her conversion, she lost interest in studying any subject but the Bible. She dropped out of school, fearing that further exposure to modernist theories such as evolution (which had been the cause of her earlier bouts of doubting) would corrupt her. There is no evidence that she ever completed high school. However, she appears to have been an avid reader and a quick study who devoured extensive written material on a variety of subjects.[7]

While her conversion had been sudden and dramatic, Aimee's call to the ministry was more protracted, with the first inkling coming shortly after her conversion with a simple period of restlessness:

> For a week, I was supremely happy. Then one day, the calm of my serenity was broken. "The whole thing is too one-sided!" I cried. Running my hands through my Bible for his answer, as was my custom, I found words like, "He that winneth souls is wise, and shall shine as the stars forever and

ever." It was as though a great voice had spoken in trumpet tones. "'Now that you, yourself, have been saved-go, help rescue others!'"[8]

This initial call was followed by an intense period of searching in which Aimee sought to discover whether there was any biblical basis to support the public ministry of women. As part of her search, she queried her parents. Her call was no surprise to her Salvationist mother, who had herself abandoned what she felt was a call to preach when she married. Minnie Kennedy struggled for some time after that with the guilt of having done so and longed for a way to square herself with God for the souls she felt called to win. One day, shortly before Aimee's birth, after reading the story of Hannah in 1 Samuel.[9] Minnie had prayed: "Lord, give me a little girl, and I will give her unreservedly into your service that she may preach the word I should have preached, fill the place I should have filled, and live the life I should have lived in Thy service."[10]

When quizzed, however, Minnie at first did not counsel her daughter to follow her call. Instead, she cautioned her about the limitations and problems she would face as a woman. Her father, James, pointed her to examples of women in scripture. He also persuaded her that there was an alternate interpretation to Paul's much-quoted passage (1 Cor. 14:34) regarding the need for women to keep silent in the congregation, having to do with ignorant women learning in silence rather than women preaching in the church.

While seeking confirmation of her call, she also sought the Holy Spirit baptism, feeling this would give her the spiritual power she needed to undertake ministry. Shortly after she began seeking, she received the experience with evidence of speaking in tongues.[11] During that same time, the young girl and the young evangelist who had led her to conversion quickly struck up a friendship, carried out mostly by

110

correspondence while he was traveling and evangelizing. He returned to ask Aimee to become his wife and join him in ministry. Eight months after her conversion, Aimee Kennedy married Robert Semple.[12]

Robert and Aimee Semple went first to Chicago in 1909 to work in William Durham's Pentecostal Mission. They were ordained together in January of that year and worked with Durham in pastoral and evangelistic work for a year and a half. In 1910, Aimee and her young husband set out on a journey as missionaries to Hong Kong, where they engaged in evangelistic work. But this excursion was tragically short-lived. Within a few months, both contracted malaria. Aimee recovered, but Robert Semple died in Hong Kong. The couple had been married only two years, but this had reportedly been the happiest period of her adult life. During that period, Aimee had come to accept the major tenets of her husband's Pentecostal faith. These tenets would become the theological backbone on which her ministry would be established.

She was pregnant at the time of Robert's death. A few months later, at the age of twenty, she returned to the United States with her new daughter, Roberta, and settled in New York. Aimee's mother joined her and the two lived and ministered for a time in the city as members of the Salvation Army. At first, McPherson's ministry consisted of attending various revival meetings and offering to help in any way possible. She took on whatever mundane tasks the leaders requested of her and participated in the worship service in whatever way she was allowed.[13]

In 1912, after two years of struggling to raise her daughter and remain active in ministry, Aimee married Harold McPherson, a wholesale grocer in Providence, Rhode Island whom she married two years later. The union got off to a rocky start and was never truly happy. Throughout its early years, Aimee renewed the struggle with her now

111

intensified call to the ministry. In 1915, one year after the marriage, she experienced an illness with symptoms including heart and nerve problems and stomach hemorrhaging. She became convinced that God would heal her if she would obey the call to preach.[14] Reportedly, as soon as she responded that she would accept the call, she was healed and within two weeks was completely well. She described the experience in her autobiography:

> My health broke, and I was taken to the hospital, where I underwent a serious major operation. Instead of improving, I grew worse. Even under ether, I could hear the Voice bidding me keep my early pledge to preach the Word.

> Finally, my condition became critical, and I was taken in to a separate room to die. A nurse sat by me in the early hours of the morning, watching my flickering pulse. Through the death silence, which was broken only by my own painful breathing, came the Voice of the Lord in trumpet tones, "NOW WILL YOU GO?"

> Lying there face to face with the Grim Reaper, I realized that I was either going into the grave or out into the field with the gospel. I made my decision and gasped out the words, "Yes-Lord-I'll-go!"

> Instantly, new life and warmth surged through my being. I was healed and... in a few days, I was up and about.[15]

That year, McPherson preached her first solo evangelistic meeting in East Providence, Rhode Island. From that time, her active evangelistic ministry throughout the United States and Canada never faltered for want of preaching engagements.

Within two years of the marriage, Harold had converted to Pentecostalism and was, at first, supportive of his wife's ministry endeavors. For a time, he helped with her ministry, serving as the advance man for campaigns and undertaking the mundane tasks a traveling ministry required. During this time, a second child, Rolf, was born in 1913. Shortly after his birth, Aimee returned to the revival circuit. Within a short time, Harold grew tired of the mobile lifestyle his wife's ministry demanded and abandoned traveling with her. He attempted to persuade his wife to settle down into a more traditional lifestyle, without success. When this failed, the couple permanently separated in 1919. The marriage ended in divorce in 1921.[16]

Aimee McPherson was a show woman from the outset and used a variety of unconventional tactics to draw and hold the crowds that gathered for her meetings. These included standing in the middle of a busy town square and pretending she was a statue, going into saloons and dance halls and taking the stage to announce that her revival meeting was in town, and dropping tracts from an airplane in a community where one of her meetings was to be held. She used whatever other tactics her fruitful imagination could cook up and she thought would gain the desired results.

From 1916 to 1918, McPherson conducted a series of tent revivals. She traveled throughout the country in an automobile on which she had plastered Bible verses and evangelistic slogans such as "Jesus Saves," "Jesus is coming soon," and "Do you know where you will spend eternity?" Along with her were her two young children and her mother, Minnie Kennedy, who filled the void that Harold McPherson had left.

In 1918, McPherson moved to Los Angeles and established her home base to provide a stable home for her children. Yet, for the next five years, she remained primarily an itinerant evangelist, traveling to major cities and small hamlets throughout the country, usually preaching to packed crowds. These campaigns often lasted for weeks at a time, were extended days or weeks beyond the originally announced timeframe, and generally resulted in strengthening faltering Pentecostal congregations as well as establishing new, independent Pentecostal congregations in the communities in which they were held. During three of those five years, McPherson held Assemblies of God credentials-from 1919 when she was ordained with that body until 1922, when she resigned the AG credentials. During that period, she was instrumental in helping several struggling Assemblies congregations, but there is no evidence that she ever sought deployment within that denomination. She never sought titles such as reverend or bishop. She was simply "Sister" to her many admirers or "Mrs. McPherson" to her equally numerous detractors. A letter to E. N. Bell, then executive chairman of the Assemblies, indicates that there were no doctrinal differences between McPherson and that body. Rather, the split resulted from a disagreement over the propriety of McPherson building Angelus Temple with funds that she had garnered through her national campaigns.[17]

While she was with the Assemblies of God, there is evidence that she was held in esteem by many of its members. For example, she received the honor of preaching the keynote sermon during the 1920 General Council. Though her tenure with that body was short-lived, Carl Brumbeck, Assemblies of God historian, noted that her influence went far beyond the actual time she spent as a member of that organization.

It was her great campaigns (before, during, and after these years) which placed innumerable council [i.e., Assemblies of God] churches on the map. Before Sister Aimee came, many

114

of the churches were but small, struggling missions in city after city. Everywhere Mrs. McPherson preached, mammoth crowds were attracted and the attention of churches and ministers was drawn to the Pentecostal message.[18]

In the five years after McPherson settled in California, she made nine trips across the United States, holding meetings in large cities and small towns. Her first international campaign was held in 1922, in Melbourne, Australia. It lasted for five months. Other campaigns took her to New Zealand, England, and numerous times, to her native Canada.

Establishing the Church of the Foursquare Gospel

The end of these evangelistic trips always brought her back to Los Angeles. It was here, in 1922, that she set up the Echo Park Evangelistic Association as the umbrella to consolidate a variety of ministry endeavors into some controllable form. The decision to establish the association came during one of her evangelistic campaigns held in Oakland, California. At the end of this three-day event, she announced her intention to form an "interdenominational team"[19] to further her evangelistic work and "circle the golden poppy state with a chain of Spirit[-filled] ministers and churches."[20] At the end of the meeting, more than one thousand people signed the statement of doctrine of the newly formed association.[21]

Although she still traveled extensively, Los Angeles remained her base and McPherson built one of the earliest megachurches in the Pentecostal movement, the 5,300-seat Angelus Temple to house that center. Built from small and large contributions solicited through preaching campaigns around the world and from her magazine, it opened on New Year's Day, 1923, completely free of debt. It was here that "Sister"—as she was known by admirers—dressed in the white

115

nurse like uniform and blue cape adapted from her earlier Salvation Army days and preached every single night and two times on Sunday for three years. It was here that she donned her legendary costumes and presented her famous illustrated, dramatized sermons that drew crowds of multiple thousands. People stood in line for hours to gain entry to each service which, at least in the early years, was full to overflowing. Often, hundreds had to be turned away.

It was also here that she held her famous healing services, for faith healing was a large part of McPherson's ministry and evangelistic campaigns. Her monthly healing services drew her largest crowds and gained the greatest notoriety for Angelus Temple and its most famous pulpiteer. Thousands regularly came to these services—some in wheelchairs, others by ambulance. They waited patiently for "Sister Aimee" to anoint them with oil and pray. Many, but not all, reported miraculous healings from a variety of diseases. According to McPherson's biographer, Mark Epstein, the American Medical Association of San Francisco approved of her healing services, calling them, "genuine, beneficial, and wonderful."[22]

McPherson's flamboyance went beyond her ministry style. Despite her early affiliation with the Assemblies of God, later some fellow Pentecostal leaders questioned whether she was truly part of the movement because her theology deviated from the classical Pentecostal tenets of the day. McPherson described her position, which was relatively ecumenical, as "middle of the road," insisting that she preached "Bible Christianity" rather than Pentecostal doctrine.

Beginning with the tenet of initial evidence of Holy Spirit baptism, staunchly believing in divine healing and advocating the Bible as being divinely inspired, she enlarged her Pentecostal theology to incorporate her doctrine of the Foursquare Gospel on which her denomination is built.[23] She purported this to be her own unique contribution to Pentecostal theology, but the foundation for this enlarged vision was

116

rooted deep in the beginnings of the Pentecostal movement itself. According to Pentecostal historian Donald Dayton, the idea of the four-fold gospel with its thematic conception of salvation, baptism of the Holy Spirit, divine healing, and the second coming of Christ is the very foundation of Pentecostal theology. Elements of this formulation are found in the theologies of both Charles Parham and Seymour's Azusa Street movement.[24] But even earlier formulations of the doctrine that McPherson claimed was divinely revealed to her were evident in the theology of A. B. Simpson, founder of the holiness group Christian and Missionary Alliance in the late nineteenth century. Simpson's theology depicted Christ as our Savior, Sanctifier, Healer, and Coming King. In 1890, Simpson authored a book, The Four-Fold Gospel, which explicated his theology.[25]

McPherson claimed that her conception was derived solely from a vision she had while preaching in an evangelistic campaign in Oakland, California, in 1922.[26] In this vision, she saw Ezekiel's vision of a man, a lion, an ox, and an eagle[27] and four symbols: the cross, the crown, the dove, and the cup.[28] She explained that these represented the regenerated church, the second coming of Christ, baptism in the Holy Spirit, and divine healing. In her words, the episode unfolded in this manner:

> God led me to speak on... Ezekiel's vision People leaned forward in expectancy and my own soul was awed as the Spirit painted in word-pictures the glorious account which Ezekiel saw. As I spoke, God revealed... that the four faces typified the four-fold ministry of the Lord Jesus Christ; in the face of the "Man "—the Savior of the world; in the face of the "Lion"—the Giver of the Holy Ghost and fire; in the face of the "Ox"—the "Great Physician" and the "Healer" of our bodies; in the face of the "Eagle"—the "Coming King of

117

Kings." A complete Gospel for body, for soul, for spirit, and for eternity... that faced squarely in every direction!... "Why, it is the Foursquare Gospel!" burst from my heart. Instantly the Spirit bore witness!

... Born aloft upon the wings of a Holy Ghost revival, the term "The Foursquare Gospel" distinguishing the message which He had given me to preach has become known around the world.[29]

While McPherson contended God revealed this formulation to her without any outside influence, there is evidence of still another source for this conception. McPherson had earlier affiliated with George Jeffries and his Elim Foursquare Gospel Alliance established in Ireland in 1915. Around that time, McPherson had collaborated with Jeffries, who held several beliefs that resonated with her later formulation.[30]

Even her ideas on divine healing deviated from the mainstream within early Pentecostalism- not so much in form as in degree. Despite the success of her healing ministry, McPherson saw herself primarily as an evangelist and her main emphasis, even in these services, was on conversion. She saw the healing services as simply a tool towards that end.[31]

McPherson was determined not to promote Pentecostalism exclusively, but what she called "Bible Christianity" and to appeal to a wider audience than other Pentecostals of her day. Fellow Pentecostals questioned how she conducted her services because she demanded a type of control that excluded the "emotional excesses" of many Pentecostal meetings, but that her detractors termed the free flow of the Holy Spirit. She limited demonstrations such as shouting (or dancing), injections of "hallelujahs" and "amens" or outbursts of glossolalia that permeated most Pentecostal meetings. Instead, along with opera and drama, worshippers were treated to a full orchestra playing a variety of music styles, including jazz-which most other Pentecostals would have found offensive.[32]

When many Pentecostals separated themselves from other groups, McPherson was intentionally ecumenical. After resigning her AG credentials, she held Baptist ordination for a time and regularly held meetings in Baptist and Methodist churches as well as Pentecostal congregations.[33] Unafraid of venturing into realms where other Pentecostals would not go—or that they shunned entirely—to preach the gospel, Broadway stages, red-light districts, and nightclubs became pulpits for her. She befriended prostitutes and others of questionable character, whom she saw as souls as much in need of the gospel message as the most upright citizen.[34]

Despite her lack of higher education, McPherson was a prolific writer and self-styled theologian who profusely used the written and spoken media of the day. In 1917, she started a monthly newsletter, *The Bridal Call*.[35] In it, she expounded her theology, encouraged her followers, reported on the successes of her ministry, and solicited financial support. Five years after launching the newsletter, she wrote her first short autobiographical work.[36] Through the years, she worked tirelessly to produce a legacy of written work, including numerous tracts, dramatized sermons, two full-length sacred operas, several shorter operettas, and numerous religious songs. Her first sacred opera, "O Worship the King," was written in 1929.

McPherson's early use of radio as a vehicle for spreading the gospel was indicative of her pioneering spirit. In 1922, as the first woman to broadcast a sermon on the radio[37] and to receive a license from the Federal Communications Commission to operate a radio station, she first secured time on one of Los Angeles' two existing stations and began to broadcast. With the license and $75,000, she set

119

up KFSG (Kalling Four Square Gospel) a year after Angelus Temple opened. The station was one of the first radio stations in the United States, as well as the first completely religious station in the country and only the third radio station to begin operation in Los Angeles. It carried her broadcast to hundreds of stations throughout the United States and Canada.

Further distinguishing herself from fellow Pentecostals, McPherson did not shy away from either social outreach or social or political activism. In 1927, she launched her social service ministry that had at its heart the Angelus Temple Commissary.[38] Daily, throughout the Depression, this ministry supplied hundreds of Los Angeles citizens with material sustenance-food, clothing, and more-necessary to cope with the problems of poverty and social distress or to merely survive. No questions were asked about church affiliation or reason for need; neither were there any conditions that had to be met before a person could receive assistance.

During the height of the Depression, in 1931, McPherson enlarged her social outreach to include a soup kitchen. She got grocery stores to contribute food and trucking companies to deliver it. She even convinced bankers and businessmen to contribute funds. In the first month of operation, the soup kitchen reportedly fed more than eighty thousand people. She persuaded the White Sewing Machine Company to contribute sewing machines for making baby blankets, for part of her ministry involved working with unwed mothers and abandoned babies. During this same period, she convinced a group of doctors and dentists to set up a free clinic and petitioned the Army to re-open an abandoned facility to house the homeless. One biographer contends that the Foursquare commissary and soup kitchen was "the most effective relief organization in the city, during those dreadful times."[39]

Within the Pentecostal realm, McPherson was socially progressive beyond her times. She continued to carry out the Azusa Street legacy of racial mixing, when others had abandoned it. Her meetings were open to and openly attended by people of all races. When she traveled to the segregated South and held meetings in white facilities that were not open to African Americans, she often held separate meetings for them. Often whites were welcomed and would come to these meetings.[40]

Her political involvement ranged from participation in local civic activities to involvement and commentary on local and national issues. Locally, involvement included such mundane activities as submitting award-winning floats from Angelus Temple for the Rose Bowl Parade. When Los Angeles was plagued with prostitution, bootlegging, dope pushers, crime, and political corruption, McPherson was an outspoken crusader for cleaning up the city. She chose, however, not to attack the political leadership directly, but to lobby for positive actions to bring about reform. Yet she was not above attacking persons she felt directly responsible for the city's moral decline and called upon converted dope addicts to testify on her radio broadcast, naming places and persons from whom they had previously purchased narcotics.[41]

On the national level, as World War II approached, McPherson geared up to help. She worked in rallies to sell more than $450,000 worth of war bonds. She also established service centers to minister to the physical and spiritual needs of servicemen and women who came through the Los Angeles area on their way to their posts of duty.

McPherson's progressive vision led her to establish one of the earliest Pentecostal Bible schools in existence.[42] Immediately following the dedication of Angelus Temple in 1923, McPherson began to address the need for trained men and women to evangelize, teach new converts, and reproduce their ministries. Only five weeks after the Temple's opening, on the morning of February 6, 1923, classes in the

Echo Park Evangelistic and Missionary Training Institute began, with an enrollment of more than one hundred students. The Institute later became the Lighthouse of International Foursquare Evangelism (L.I.F.E.) Bible College and was instrumental in the Foursquare denomination coming into being. L.I.F.E. was successful in training thousands of young men and women for evangelistic ministry. Once they completed the course of study, they were sent to the "mission field" and numerous congregations sprang up because of their efforts. By 1927, graduates from L.I.F.E. were not only planting churches across the United States and Canada, but also in Africa, Latin America, and Asia.[43]

McPherson did not set out to establish a denomination. However, along with congregations established by L.I.F.E. graduates, new congregations were planted as a result of converts won in her evangelistic campaigns. Additionally, as some existing congregations were strengthened by her campaigns, they brought themselves under her aegis. The decision to become a denomination came in 1926,[44] when Minnie Kennedy had left the organization after one of the famous brawls between the two women and McPherson decided to reorganize. She began by appointing a field agent, John Goben, to organize the branch churches into "lighthouses." Standing congregations that had any loose affiliation with McPherson were also invited to formalize their relationship with Foursquare.

McPherson maintained friendships with many notable people in both the religious and secular worlds. Religious alliances included Homer Rodeheaver[45] the revivalist and prolific camp meeting songwriter who was associated with Billy Sunday; prominent evangelical preacher and writer Oswald J. Smith[46] and noted evangelist and religious broadcaster Paul Rader.[47] She also counted among her friends William Jennings Bryan,[48] three-time nominee of the Democratic Party for U.S. president and secretary of state under

122

Woodrow Wilson, who championed the biblical creationist position in the famous Scopes trial. McPherson carried on a prolonged correspondence with Bryan, a committed Christian and an eloquent speaker who occasionally preached in Angelus Temple.

She counted movie stars among those regularly attended Angelus Temple's services and involved themselves in her ministry. Anthony Quinn played saxophone in the church band as a teenager.[49] Charlie Chaplin designed sets for her illustrated gospel messages.[50] H. L. Mencken was a close friend.[51] *The New Yorker* magazine sent high-level writers such as Paxton Hibben[52] and Dorothy Parker[53] to cover her New York meetings.

Legacy of Controversy

McPherson's penchant for controversy is infamous. She was no sooner dislodged from one personal, familial, or legal situation before in the middle of another. The press relied on her to keep its gossip columns full. One aspect of her life escaped scrutiny-her love-hate relationship with the Ku Klux Klan. That relationship began with a mysterious abduction to a Klan meeting after one of her revival services. In that meeting, local Klan members commended McPherson and pledged support for her ministry. On other occasions, she accepted money from the Klan and preached to them in secluded meetings. Yet, on more than one occasion, she also openly challenged their racist beliefs and secretiveness, for her association with the Klan did not stem from common notions of race superiority, but from a shared "fundamentalist" interpretation of religion and morality that supported prohibition, stood against socialism and communism, and valued "old-fashioned" morality.[54]

Another group with which McPherson maintained a unique alliance was the gypsies. This relationship began when McPherson successfully prayed for the healing of a gypsy chief's respiratory disease

123

and his mother's fibroid tumor in her Denver meeting in 1922. After that, the gypsy chieftain pledged McPherson his undying loyalty and support and spread the news of the healing among the gypsy communities throughout the country. He urged other gypsies to attend McPherson's services, and, more importantly, he encouraged them to support her financially, and did so himself.

From that point on, when McPherson traveled to hold her tent revivals and public meetings, the gypsies from communities as far as several hundred miles away flocked to her meetings. They often pitched tent cities around the main tent or building and stayed for the duration of the meeting. They contributed substantially to the building of Angelus Temple, and hundreds of gypsies became members or regular attendees.

The most controversial episode in McPherson's life involved a three-week disappearance in May 1926 and the subsequent charges and counter-charges that grew out of it.[55] While sunbathing on a local beach with her secretary, McPherson suddenly vanished. She was presumed dead by followers, but just as suddenly reappeared a month later, maintaining she had been kidnapped and taken to Mexico, but escaped and found her way back home. Some detractors,[56] however, maintained that she was involved in a romantic tryst for that period. This case went to a grand jury;[57] a separate case against McPherson for perjury also received a grand jury hearing. In the end, the district attorney did not have enough evidence to try McPherson and charges were dropped. Yet, this episode signaled a turning point in her ministry. The public remained divided over the truth of the episode, the integrity of her life, and the viability of her ministry. Supporters were convinced her story was true or the episode was inconsequential and still came in large numbers to meetings. Her detractors saw it as another indication of her instability. The press, which up until this point had been generally friendly or mostly curious, began to take a more suspicious attitude toward McPherson and her antics.

In 1930, she suffered what was characterized as a nervous breakdown, partly due to the strain of the trial.[58] She was hospitalized for a brief time and subsequently experienced recurring periods of insomnia, nervousness, and agitation. But this was only the beginning of a continuing downward spiral for McPherson's health. The next major controversy arose over her 1931 elopement and marriage to Angelus Temple choir member David Hutton.[59] This marriage lasted only three- and one-half years, ending in divorce early in 1935. Detractors were quick to point out the inconsistency between McPherson's personal actions and the Pentecostal prohibition against remarriage of divorcees with living ex-spouses. Again, her most avid followers were quick to forgive. During the marriage, McPherson asserted that she had biblical warrant for the marriage since Harold McPherson had divorced her. Yet, after the divorce, McPherson amended the doctrinal statement of the Foursquare Church to include a clause against the remarriage of persons with a living ex-spouse.[60]

Throughout her public ministry, she, and the female family members (her mother, Minnie Kennedy, and daughter Roberta), kept themselves in the public eye through a series of public disputes that found their way to the press. The culmination of these controversies was a loss of standing among some supporters who had backed her in her heyday. Several of the churches that had affiliated with the new denomination dropped out of the fellowship. Other leaders ceased inviting her to their meetings. But the faithful continued to give their support.

The only major split in the denomination came in 1932, when thirty-two ministers withdrew in reaction to publicity about McPherson and her mother and "certain Foursquare policies" that were being instituted. They formed the Open Bible Evangelistic

Association.[61] In 1935, the group merged with another organization, the Bible Standard Churches of America, to form the Open Bible Standard Churches.[62] The constituency of that organization never grew to more than twenty-one hundred churches and one hundred thousand members, primarily in the Midwest,[63] while McPherson's organization grew to be at least twenty times that size.

The final controversy revolved around McPherson's death in 1944 at the age of fifty-three from an overdose of prescribed sleeping pills. Like most episodes of her life, supporters and detractors debated the circumstances of her death. But the final coroner's report ruled her death an accident.

Ministry and Leadership of Women

Neither her social progressiveness nor her penchant for controversy led her to publicly champion the cause of women preachers or become embroiled in the discussions of women's roles in the church and public ministry. It appears that this simply was not her issue and she largely ignored public debate about it, choosing instead to deliberately, and conspicuously, go about doing whatever she felt called to do. According to one description of her failure to engage the issue: "She placed more emphasis on motherhood than on her independence as a single woman, but there was little attention paid to either topic in her autobiographical writings. Neither did she make much of her gender or of women's rights, so it is difficult to argue that she viewed her religious work in a feminist way. Nor do programs of the Foursquare Gospel appear to have any distinctly feminist concerns."[64] On one occasion when she was directly questioned about whether or not she liked to hear a woman preach, she replied, "No! Neither do I like to hear a man preach. But I love to hear God speak, whether the vessel is a woman or a man."[65]

126

Several times throughout her ministry, however, she made statements supporting women's ministry and placed the Foursquare movement solidly in favor of their right to preach the gospel. On one occasion, she remarked about the denomination's openness to women:

This is the only church, I am told, that is ordaining women preachers. The A[ssemblies of] G[od] are not ordaining women to my knowledge Four squaredom is the only work that has given such acknowledgment to women preachers as well as men.

Even the Pentecostal works in some cases have said "No women preachers!" But I am opening the door, and as long as Sister McPherson is alive, she is going to hold the door open and say, ladies, come![66]

In a Bible class she taught at Angelus Temple on the book of Acts, she once took a rare opportunity to comment specifically on the scriptural warrant from the passage in Act 2:17-18 for a woman's right to preach: "When God anoints you to preach, here are your credentials and authority, students, whether male or female: 'Your sons and daughters shall prophesy.' When people say a woman should not preach in church, remember, thus saith the Scripture?"[67]

At another time, in a commentary in Bridal Call, on the Joel 2:28 passage, McPherson argued, "Before the coming of the Lord takes place there must be at least a few women preaching the gospel—else the scripture will not be fulfilled. [68]

McPherson was just as articulate in defending her own right to public ministry. "Don't tell me that a woman cannot be called to preach the gospel," she said on one occasion. "If any man went through one-hundredth part of the hell on earth that I lived in those months when [I was] out of God's will and work, they would never say that again."[69]

McPherson's words belied her own actions concerning women, which were mixed at best. She used both women and men in her ministry; her primary criterion for choosing leaders was her perception of their capacity to advance herself and her organization. Yet, despite lack of direct affirmation, many women were drawn to McPherson as a role model and leader and were involved in almost every aspect of her ministry-including, initially, the leadership of the organization. McPherson ordained women as ministers, appointed them to pastorates and the L.I.F.E. Bible College faculty, and sent them out as missionaries and church planters.[70]

Yet, McPherson's convoluted stand on gender equality resulted in many jobs at Angelus Temple being gender-specific. Only men served as ushers and elders; only women served on the greeting committee or as deacons. These titles suggest, moreover, that though they worked in similar arenas, men generally had slightly more responsibility and authority than women. And importantly, though several women worked closely with McPherson in her organization, no women were allowed in the pulpit at Angelus Temple when she was present.[71]

The relationships McPherson held with the women who worked closely with her were often complicated. Chief among these women was her mother, Minnie Kennedy. During her early evangelistic campaigns, Kennedy served as her constant companion on road trips as well as her babysitter, confidant, and advisor. Kennedy and McPherson are believed to be the first two women to travel alone by automobile across the entire United States. Through McPherson's early ministry years, Kennedy was by her side, handling vital functions that made McPherson's ministry run smoothly. She acted as front woman on their travels, when Harold declined to do so. She cared for the children, took care of housekeeping chores, and provided camaraderie on a circuit that often proved to be very lonely. In later years, Kennedy served as McPherson's business manager, managing the Temple's financial matters and correspondences while handling Bridal Call subscriptions and backstage details for McPherson's numerous engagements. Her frugal financial management is credited with allowing the organization to save the five thousand dollars used to begin the Angelus Temple project.[72]

Although her mother remained her confidante and close companion, with McPherson, at one point, proclaiming, "she has ever been the source of cheer and inspiration,"[73] the two women had a convoluted and often volatile relationship that resulted in at least one public physical altercation that received press notoriety. It finally ended after that 1930 episode and Kennedy received a cash settlement from her daughter in return for relinquishing all rights to the business affairs of Angelus Temple and the Echo Park Evangelistic Association. Any contact between the two after that was either through newspaper reports, lawyers, or their common ally, McPherson's daughter, Roberta.

Another woman working closely with McPherson was Harriet Jordan.[74] Jordan had been healed in one of McPherson's 1921 revival meetings. She served in one capacity or another on the Temple staff from its opening in 1923. Around 1930, Jordan temporarily took charge of the Temple and was the business manager. She handled the ministerial affairs at Angelus Temple during McPherson's many road tours. She was one of the first students to graduate from and later served as dean of L.I.F.E. Bible School, from 1929 to 1942. During her tenure as dean, the school grew from two hundred to one thousand students.[75]

Rheba Crawford served as McPherson's assistant pastor for just one year—from 1935 to 1936—when the board of elders demanded the termination of her contract. Almost from the beginning, the two

129

strong-willed, outspoken women had problems.[76] Crawford's contract with Angelus Temple specified that when McPherson was on the road, Crawford would occupy the pulpit and manage the radio broadcasts.

Whenever McPherson returned to Los Angeles, Crawford was expected to leave Los Angeles and go on the preaching circuit.[77] The two women had very different styles; while McPherson was intentionally apolitical and courted a good relationship with city officials, Crawford used her radio broadcasts to rail against what she saw as corrupt city politics and at one point called for a recall of the mayor and city council. She was often in contention with others on the Temple staff. When the board asked for her resignation, Crawford subsequently sued McPherson for eighteen counts of slander and demanded one million dollars. The case was ultimately settled out of court.[78]

One of McPherson's most intriguing relationships was with her daughter, Roberta. It was in part Roberta's illness during an influenza epidemic that convinced Aimee to settle down in California and have a home base for her ministry rather than continue as a traveling evangelist. Partly because Roberta was Robert Semple's daughter whom McPherson saw as born to carry out her late father's legacy, Aimee had always intended her to succeed as pastor of Angelus Temple and was training her to do so. According to McPherson, "It had always been understood in my family that if Jesus should tarry and my hands would grow weak, I would pass the work on to Roberta. She was to be my successor."[79]

From the time she was a young girl, Roberta was involved in McPherson's ministry. As a teenager, she led children's services every Sunday. For a time in the 1920s, while still in her teens, she had a radio broadcast for children, and she wrote children's columns for *Bridal Call* magazine. She served for a period as the vice president and business

130

manager for Angelus Temple but showed no interest in taking over the organization's leadership.

In 1930, at the age of twenty, she married a ship's steward. Her young husband found her mother's antics strange and did not support his wife's involvement with her. That marriage lasted for only three years, but during that time, Roberta paid less attention to the ministry.[80] When the marriage ended, in 1933, she returned to the ministry for a short while, but working with her mother became increasingly difficult. In 1941, Roberta married NBC radio music director and bandleader Harry Salter.[81] They moved to New York, where Roberta used her creative talent to collaborate with her husband in producing game shows.

Before her marriage and move, Roberta had been one of many litigators against her mother, taking McPherson's lawyer to court over allegations of impropriety with Temple administrative policy and winning the suit. McPherson and her daughter severed relations in 1943, and from that time until McPherson's death in 1944, despite Roberta's attempts to reach her mother by mail and telephone, there were no communications between the two.[82]

Whether McPherson intended to further the cause of women, or not, one action-establishing the Bible Institute, which became L.I.F.E. Bible College, and opening its doors equally to men and women- had a far-reaching effect on the ministry of women within the Foursquare church. Three-fourths of the first students in the Foursquare Training Institute were women and fourteen of the first sixteen graduates were women. The establishing of L.I.F.E. Bible College figured into furthering the ministry of women in another way. Through its affiliation with Angelus Temple, it provided a laboratory for them to practice their preaching skills. McPherson often allowed young men and women from the Bible College to take center pulpit and preach in the Friday night "Crusader Services" that were dedicated to young people. As they tried out their sermonic styles, she would sit on the sidelines, encouraging them.[83]

During the early years, women as well as men- most of them recent graduates of L.I.F.E. Bible School-were instrumental in the early spread of the Foursquare movement, planting new congregations or "branches" throughout the United States and Canada. They served as church planters and pastors, evangelists, and missionaries. Many of these women were later appointed to positions of leadership throughout the organization.

An example of such a woman is Anna Britton, a close friend and ministerial assistant of McPherson. For a time, she worked as part of the administrative staff of the Temple and part of the ministerial support team. She was responsible for training altar workers, and along with Crawford and Jordan, occasionally preached at the Temple when McPherson had to be absent. Britton planted churches in Santa Ana, Long Beach, Santa Monica, and Pasadena, California. She then went on to start a Bible Institute in Vancouver, British Columbia, which became Pacific L.I.F.E. Bible College.[84]

Other outstanding examples include Evelyn Taylor, who planted congregations in Missouri, and later served as superintendent of the state. Louise Webster planted a thriving church in Phoenix, Arizona, and was later appointed superintendent of that state. Isabell Hall, who became the architect for the Foursquare Christian education program, had previously planted congregations in Minneapolis, Roanoke, Virginia, Iowa, and Urbana, Illinois. Helen Granvoll was a missionary to Panama who had planted a congregation in Santa Ana, California.[85] Another group of women McPherson involved in her ministry was the "City Sisters."[86] These mostly affluent housewives voluntarily staffed the commissary and social outreach ministries of the Temple. They were not ordained ministers, but lay women whose involvement had many elements of the more mundane ladies' ministry projects of less progressive churches. However, they also functioned as spiritual leaders, regularly involved in evangelism, praying, and sharing the gospel with each person to whom they provided material substance.[87] Another lay ministry in which women were heavily involved was in manning the twenty-four-hour prayer tower. Two-thirds of the people who ministered there were women.

Legacy for Women

Again, whether she intentionally made the furtherance of women's ministries a part of her effort or not, her example of extraordinary leadership and utilization of women in strategic roles within the Foursquare movement inspired women in Foursquare to levels of leadership unattainable in most other Pentecostal denominations. From its foundation, women have been fully ordained and may serve as pastors as well as in elected or appointed leadership roles at every level of the church. In the early years, nearly 40 percent of Foursquare pastors were women. Blumhofer notes specifically that in 1927—three years after the founding of the Evangelistic Association—eighteen of the fifty-five branch churches were headed by a female, another two had female associate pastors, and sixteen were headed by married couples as copastors. However, the actual participation of women in the ministry and leadership of the International Church of the Foursquare Gospel continued to decline throughout McPherson's lifetime so that by the time of her death only 16 percent of pastors were female.[88]

Eventually, in 1937, McPherson put control of the Temple's business into the hands of her son, Rolf, and Giles Knight; denominational leadership has remained in the hands of men since that time. However, the denomination publicly takes an egalitarian stand on the issue of the ministry and leadership of women. In 1975, the Annual Convention adopted the brief "Denominational Statement Regarding

Women in Public Ministry." It stated, "A close study of the Word of God... indicates that God has seen fit to use women in His service in virtually every way He has employed men. We... see nothing that should restrict the God-ordained and Spirit-filled ministry of women in any capacity or office of the Church in keeping with the Word of God which guides men and women alike."[89]

In 1988, the board of directors unanimously passed a declaration that read: "The... position of the Foursquare Church affirms the Biblical Truth that women are called of God to roles of leadership and public ministry. We hereby affirm and encourage the ministry of women throughout the International Church of the Foursquare Gospel."[90]

A later position paper on the subject developed specifically to "answer a consistent stream of inquiries as to the Foursquare Church's attitude towards the biblical rights of women to serve in ministry and leadership, even to the extent of holding ecclesiastical position" contains the following affirmation: "The International Church of the Foursquare Gospel affirms the place of women in ordained ministry and leadership. This belief affords women positions in all capacities in the local church, on the mission field and at all levels of government."[91]

Today, the vast majority of Foursquare officers are male; all top positions are held by males and only a fraction of solo senior pastors are female.[92] Yet the denomination has the unique practice of ordaining and appointing husband and wife pastoral teams, thereby affording women a greater opportunity for ministerial input and leadership than is available in most other Pentecostal bodies. At the same time, this practice inflates the numerical reality of women who serve in pastoral roles, since at least some, if not most, of the women in these paired teams take on the role of assistant pastor to their husband's role as senior pastor. This is sometimes reversed, with the woman taking on the senior pastor role.[93]

134

At her death, McPherson's legacy was a denomination with more than four hundred "lighthouses" established throughout the United States and Canada, two hundred missionaries stationed throughout the world, approximately twenty-nine thousand members, and assets valued at nearly three million dollars. Since then, the Foursquare church has grown to be the most viable of the four denominations and the only one of the four that is counted as one of the thirty-eight major U.S. Pentecostal bodies. The Foursquare Church is the fifth largest of Pentecostal denominations, behind the organization out of which McPherson came, the Assemblies of God, the predominantly African American Church of God in Christ, the Church of God, and the oneness United Pentecostal Church. Indeed, it stands as the largest denomination started by a woman within all of Christian history. McPherson's only rival for this distinction is the Church of Christ Scientist, founded by Mary Baker Eddy in the nineteenth century, which has some two million members in two thousand churches in sixty countries.[94]

As of 2003, there were 1,888 congregations and nearly 251,614 members of the Foursquare Church in the United States. Most are concentrated on the West Coast, but there are Foursquare churches in all fifty states. Additionally, there are more than thirty thousand congregations and nearly 3.5 million members in 123 countries worldwide. Along with L.I.F.E. Bible College in Los Angeles, there are more than two hundred Bible schools in eighty-three countries.[95]

McPherson's flamboyant ministry was not unnoticed by even secular media. Several fictional works are based, at least in part, on her life. Perhaps the most well-known is Elmer Gantry, the 1927 Sinclair Lewis work made into a movie in 1960. In 1931, Barbara Stanwyck starred in The Miracle Woman. Her character, Susan Fallon, seems to have been derived from McPherson's life and the Gantry storyline. Forty years later, McPherson's story still fascinated audiences. The

1975 production of the 1927 Nathaniel West novel Day of the Locust added a female evangelist who incorporates showiness and faith healing.[96] That same year, a Hallmark Hall of Fame television production, The Disappearance of Aimee, was broadcast nationally. Additionally, stories of McPherson's life and the controversies surrounding it appeared in such mainstream magazines as *The New Yorker*, *Time Magazine*, *Vanity Fair*, and *Harper's* throughout the 1920s, '30s and '40s.[97] Some of these questioned her morality and integrity. Others, such as the *Vanity Fair* paper doll cut-up caption that described her as "Aimee Semple McPherson Hutton, the Vanishing Evangelist who takes hikes, world jaunts, and husbands, all in the name of faith," simply made fun of her.[98] Even sixty years after her death, she still graced the pages of national publications as journalists attempted to discern her unique place in American religious history. Noted author Upton Sinclair memorialized her disappearance in poetry.[99] Such notable periodicals as *Christian History* and special interest publications such as Opera, geared to the serious music community, dealt with her legacy.[100] As late as 1999, a documentary on National Public Radio included interviews with her daughter, Roberta, and her son, Rolf.[101]

Conclusion

Aimee Semple McPherson holds a place in history as one of the most famous women in modern Pentecostal and American religious history. She comes to that place by having founded the largest Christian denomination (of any tradition) founded by a woman. Sources regarding McPherson's life and ministry, her famous and infamous antics, and the atmosphere of controversy that constantly surrounded her, are prolific. Unfortunately, however, information regarding her specific contribution to furthering the ministry and leadership of women is not easily assessable since the voluminous materials that are available do not directly focus on McPherson's contribution to the leadership of women in the Pentecostal movement.

There are several reasons for this disparity. First, McPherson did not often write or speak publicly about the issue of women's position because this was not the focus of her attention. She saw no need to defend the public ministry of women in general or herself in particular. McPherson's energies were completely focused on spreading the gospel, winning souls, and administering healing to those in spiritual, physical, mental, emotional, and material distress. Her life and accomplishments in these areas were her defense.

Second, McPherson's evangelistic style of ministry, with its inherent charismatic gifts, was welcomed by both men and women within the early sectarian Pentecostal milieu, in which charismatic leadership was the norm. Her demonstrated ability to preach a sermon that could hold the attention of large crowds for several hours and her demonstrated success in praying for the sick to receive healing ensured her a place on the Pentecostal revival circuit.

McPherson did not start out to create a new organization but rather saw herself as an evangelist. In this role, she was not a threat to any hierarchical structure. Within this role, she found a niche for herself within the limited liberty that was provided for early Pentecostal women. Within that niche, she created a ministry that touched hundreds of thousands of lives, made thousands of converts and reached around the world.

Even as she built her Evangelistic Association, McPherson did not intentionally set out to build a denomination. As her Angelus Temple congregation grew to several thousand members, she still considered herself an evangelist—a preacher of the gospel to the lost-not a pastor of those who were already Christian. She began her ministry traveling throughout Canada and the United States to hold revival meetings, preaching her unique brand of middle-of-the-road Christianity (with a

Pentecostal twist) among Baptists and Methodists as we'll as Pentecostals. Even when she preached at Angelus Temple services filled to capacity with more than five thousand worshippers, she was still essentially an evangelist. In 1931, for example, eight years after the opening of Angelus Temple, she was on the revival circuit, conducting a fifteen-thousand-mile, twenty-one-state tour that lasted several months. During that tour, she preached more than three hundred sermons in nearly fifty cities, reaching a million people.[102]

By sheer example, McPherson demonstrated what a woman consumed by vision could do. She inspired hundreds of women to consider the ministry. But she did not stop there. First, through the Bible Training School, then through L.I.F.E. Bible College and affiliates, she provided the mechanism to prepare them to assume any role to which they felt called. At a time when seminary education was primarily a male bastion, she opened the doors of her Bible school to men and women. Women graduates of these institutions were regularly sent out to pastorates and mission stations, in numbers equal to, and sometimes exceeding, their male colleagues.

The third reason the impact of McPherson's legacy has been lessened is that her antics and the controversy that continued to surround her constantly overshadowed any contribution she would have made to whatever cause she might have taken on. Pentecostals who took seriously their holiness roots, with its emphasis on personal piety, were put off by her antics, three marriages, and constant involvement in litigation. Even when they did not openly condemn her, they would not have used her as a role model. Some within the movement dismissed her as an immoral, self-seeking phony, willing to compromise the gospel for her own gratification. Others saw her as an eccentric oddity, good for a show, but not to be taken seriously. Because of this, the impact that her accomplishments might have had on Pentecostal women certainly was less than it otherwise might have been.

Another factor that mitigated her contribution to furthering the leadership of women within Pentecostalism was the reality that her relationships with women were convoluted. Even the women she trusted and depended on most could not maintain a consistent relationship with her. This was fueled partly by her almost paranoid distrust of everyone around her. And she seemed to trust the women in her life less than she trusted the men. Even the two women closest to her—her mother and daughter—finally broke off their relationships with her. And, importantly, no woman ever preached in the Sunday worship service or in the regular weekly services at Angelus Temple when McPherson was present, even though she had several women with preaching skills that rivaled her own on her ministerial staff.

Despite limitations, her greatest contribution to Pentecostal women's leadership and ministry is what she accomplished. By reasonable standards, Aimee McPherson was successful in building a worldwide organization that has flourished and grown over the six decades since her death. To this day, that organization—the International Church of the Foursquare Gospel—maintains a place for the ministry and leadership of women that, though somewhat limited, is unequaled within Pentecostalism.

Ida Robinson
Mt. Sinai Holy Church Of America, Inc.

Ida Robinson holds the distinction of being the founder of the largest African American Pentecostal denomination established by a woman and continually headed by women.[1] She is also thus distinguished as establishing the largest denomination headed by an African American woman. This double distinction comes to her as the visionary leader of Mt. Sinai Holy Church of America, Inc., a body that from its beginnings promoted the equality and leadership of women in Pentecostal ministry.

Early Life and Ministry

Ida Bell was born August 3, 1891, in Hazlehurst, Georgia, in the southeastern portion of the state. She was the seventh of twelve children of Robert and Annie Bell. Sometime during her early childhood, the family moved to Pensacola, Florida, where she spent the rest of her youth. We know little of the familial, educational, or cultural influences that shaped her early life, but her biographers estimate that she attained only a fourth-grade education, at best. We know that she was reared in the segregated South during the height of the Jim Crow period—a time in which educational and cultural opportunities for African Americans were extremely limited. We also know that during this period, the black church held a central position in the life and well-being of these communities. Ida Robinson is part of the legacy of the black church.

We do not know her early religious affiliation. However, even as a child, Ida Bell was known for her religious zeal. During her teen years, she was converted at a street meeting in Pensacola conducted by a local congregation of the Church of God (Cleveland, Tenn.). Almost immediately, Ida's lifelong vocation as a preacher and evangelist began

141

to unfold as she involved herself in holding prayer meetings in her home and in other homes in the surrounding community. She also began holding street services and preaching on street corners to anyone who would pay attention. Her sermons drew crowds who listened intently as she expounded on her newfound faith. Even as a young woman, Ida was showing signs of the dynamic gifts that would repeatedly be used to bring people to belief in Christ and, later, to draw members to her organization.

As a young woman, Ida worked as a cook on a tugboat near Miami while carrying out her ministry on the side. She married Oliver Robinson in 1909 at the age of eighteen. Since little is recorded of her personal life, not much is known about their marital relationship. It is known that the two of them continued to work on the tugboat until 1917, when they moved from Florida to Philadelphia at the urging of Ida's sister, who had earlier migrated there.[2] Like hundreds of thousands of African Americans who were going North in the early twentieth-century urban migration, they were seeking more stable and lucrative jobs and a greater degree of racial freedom than they could find in the South. By the time Robinson left Florida, although she was only twenty-six years old, she had already established several neighborhood prayer groups, which she left behind.[3]

Ida and Oliver maintained a solid marital relationship that continued until Ida's death in 1946. Though Oliver was a lifelong member of her congregation, he never took an active role in ministry or leadership. However, he appeared to be supportive of Ida, serving as her driver, to her many speaking engagements.[4] Old-timers remember his public praise of his wife's "spiritual endeavors" as well as his provision of the necessary support in the home to make sure she was free to do ministry.[5] The couple had no children, but adopted and raised Ida's nine-year-old niece—also named Ida Bell—whom she referred to as her daughter.

Little is known of the initial involvement of Robinson's immediate family in her ministry. But her extended family played a major role in building her organization. Nieces and nephews, grandnieces and nephews are evident throughout the organization, as the name Bell continues to surface in various locations. A glaring omission in all of the information concerning Robinson's ministry and family is any reference to the ongoing relationship between Robinson and her adopted daughter especially as related to the younger woman's involvement in the Mt. Sinai organization. It appears that theirs remained a warm relationship. However, at the same time, presumably after the older woman's death, the younger Ida left the Mt. Sinai organization.

After moving to Philadelphia, Robinson was affiliated with a local congregation of the Church of God for two years. During that time, she assisted the pastor in preaching and other leadership responsibilities. Her ministry again included holding street evangelistic meetings and home Bible studies. She also filled in for the pastor in the pulpit when he was absent and reportedly was popular with other members of the congregation. There is some indication that her popularity might have been a problem for this pastor, for Robinson is said to have left the congregation in 1919, after an "uncomfortable situation" arose.[6]

Whether or not this uncomfortable situation arose because of jealousy on the part of the pastor, it might have come about because of the increasing restrictions that the Church of God had already begun to place on women. By 1919, the Church of God had made its decision precluding women from being ordained, from performing the sacraments, and from taking part in the business and government of the local congregations and the General Assembly.

143

Establishing Mt. Sinai Holy Church

When Robinson left the Church of God at the age of twenty-eight, she moved to Mt. Olive Holy Church. There she was ordained to the ministry by Elder Henry Fisher, the president of the United Holy Church. Shortly after Robinson moved to that congregation, the pastor died, and Robinson was appointed pastor.[7] A year later, the Mt. Olive Holy Church was one of the founding congregations of the Northern District of the United Holy Church of America.[8]

Despite having little formal education, Robinson was lauded by her followers for having a sharp intellect and excellent leadership skills, as well as being a "keen student of the Bible."[9] She was a gifted preacher and singer, and people who came to hear her sing and preach regularly filled her church. Many of these visitors stayed to become members, thus fueling the expansion of the congregation. So, while still a part of the United Holy Church, the congregation grew rapidly under Robinson's leadership, having to move to new facilities three times because it had outgrown the space it occupied.[10]

Along with her work in her local congregation, Robinson enjoyed an active evangelistic ministry. By 1924, though she remained largely obscure to the wider society, her reputation as a singer and as a preaching revivalist had spread up and down the eastern African American Pentecostal circuit. She regularly traveled from New York to North Carolina preaching, singing, and baptizing new converts.

Robinson's giftedness was apparent not only to rank-and-file Pentecostal believers, but also to Male and female colleagues in the ministry and the United Holy Church leadership. Fisher and other leaders often called on her to assist them in their evangelistic meetings, to sing one of her special selections, exhort the congregation before the main sermon, or pray with those who came to the altar after the sermon seeking prayer for salvation, sanctification, Holy Spirit baptism, or healing. Because of her many gifts and the following she

144

had established, she would probably have had a secure position with the United Holy Church. But Robinson heard a higher calling.

Even though she was useful to United Holy Church leadership, her gifts and reputation proved to be problematic because, though, in the early 1920s, women outnumbered men in the denomination by two to one, women preachers were almost unheard of. Due in part to her success and example, women within the United Holy Church began to pursue the ministry and demand a more active and public role in the denomination's leadership.[11]

In response, the largely male United Holy Church leadership began to question women's roles as pastors and finally took a stance that proved precipitous to Robinson's decision to leave. In 1924, Fisher and G. J. Branch, his vice president, announced that they would no longer "publicly" ordain women to the ministry.[12] Additionally, those women who had already been ordained were restricted to serve in only the lower levels of ordained ministry. As Cheryl Townsend Gilkes states, "women could elect bishops, but could not be bishops."[13]

The seriousness with which Robinson took their action resulted in her decision to seek God for resolution of the problem. Their announcement convinced her to undertake ten days of fasting and prayer regarding the situation of women preachers in the United Holy Church. Fasting is a standard part of Pentecostal spirituality, and many Pentecostals regularly fast for short periods. Robinson, however, willingly took on ten days of denying herself food and sustenance to put herself in the spiritual position to petition God for divine direction, assistance, or, perhaps, intervention in the matter.

Already open to frequent dreams and visions to gain God's leading in her life, during this time, she had a series of dreams that she felt were God's mechanism for answering her prayers. After the fasting period ended, she declared that God was telling her to leave the organization

145

and to start a new denomination, and she promptly set the wheels in motion to do so.[14]

Not wanting to lose such a gifted individual and realizing the seriousness of her intentions, United Holy Church leaders tried to change her mind. She refused their overtures, reportedly responding that God had instructed her to "Come out on Mt. Sinai and loose the women."[15] She perceived this summons as a direct command to start a new organization that would promote the full ministry of women. She questioned, "If Mary the mother of Jesus could carry the word of God in her womb, why can't women carry the word of God in their mouth?"[16]

No record recounts the specific details of the imagery of Mt. Sinai in the dreams Robinson experienced. Neither did she follow the examples of Tate and McPherson in providing elaborate detail of the distinctive meaning of the organization's title. But since the Mt. Sinai name came about in response to Robinson's claimed directive from God, its meaning holds a significant key to what Robinson saw herself doing in founding the new organization. In Hebrew Scripture, Mt. Sinai (or alternately, Mt. Horeb) was the place where Moses encountered God. It is here that God delivered the laws that are called the Ten Commandments.

God called the biblical hero Moses to lead the children of Israel out of Egyptian bondage to freedom in Canaan-the promised land. Robinson saw herself equally called by God to lead women out of the bondage of the United Holy Church to a place of freedom in ministry in her new organization. So the theme of the one called out on the mountain by God to lead prophetically an unjustly treated people became the foundation for her sense of mission and provided the name for her new organization.

The imagery of Mary, as a woman bearer of the incarnate Word of God, gave Robinson further biblical support for her mission. She equated Mary's divinely appointed mission as no less compelling than the mission women had been given to carry the spoken word to those around them. The irony of God's choice of this lowly woman as the person to carry out one of the most important missions in salvation history was enough to dispel any critique of God's choice of Pentecostal women as carriers of the gospel message.

Based solely on what she considered a direct admonition from God, Robinson intentionally set out to provide a venue for women to develop and use their ministry and leadership skills at every level of the church without limitation. To do this, she immediately sought out legal counsel to set up the corporate structure for the Mt. Sinai Holy Church of America, Inc. Robinson's intention from the beginning was to start a new body or denomination, not just a congregation. Within three months after her fast, the structure was in place and the Mt. Sinai organization was chartered by the state of Pennsylvania. With the charter in hand, Robinson and her group were able to organize new churches and ordain the ministers needed to lead them.

The Mt. Olive congregation that Robinson was pastoring at this time became the "mother church", the first congregation and headquarters in the new organization. Many of the members of the congregation stayed with the new group, which retained ownership of the building in which they were worshipping. The second congregation came about almost immediately after she received the charter. Robinson was preaching to a group of followers in Burgaw, North Carolina, when news reached her that the charter had been granted. With her newly bestowed authority, she immediately organized the followers she had gained there and established the first church outside of her own Mt. Olive congregation.

Although she left the United Holy Church, Robinson remained friendly with its leaders.[17] Since the break was primarily over the ministry of women and not any issue of polity or doctrine, Robinson

147

saw no need to sever ties or develop a completely new polity. As a result, she patterned much of the polity and doctrine of the Mt. Sinai organization on that of the United Holy Church. She also incorporated elements from the Church of God with which she had earlier been affiliated.

When Robinson pulled her Mt. Olive congregation out of the United Holy Church, several supporters went with her. Along with the members of her congregation, many of the women earlier rejected for ordination by the United Holy Church followed Robinson into her new organization, as did some of the male and female pastors and their congregations that were sympathetic to Robinson's stand and the step she was taking to correct what she saw as an unjust situation.[18] Several of these congregations permanently realigned themselves with her so that at its first convocation in September 1924, one year after the denomination was founded, the seventeen congregations included several that had come from the United Holy Church.[19]

Even though her future in the United Holy Church would probably have been secure, Robinson's intention in starting her movement was specifically to establish an organization in which every woman minister would have full freedom to participate in every level of ministry, and in which women would have full clergy rights, including the right to ordination as bishop. Accordingly, every action she took as head of the newly formed denomination reflected this commitment and intention.

Robinson remained the pastor of Mt. Olive and the congregation served as the mother church of the new movement for some time. In 1925, the congregation purchased a two-thousand-seat edifice from an Assemblies of God congregation in Philadelphia. Eventually, however, she moved the mother church from Philadelphia to Bethel in New York City, where it remained during her lifetime.[20] For the rest of her life, she served as pastor of both congregations, dividing her time

148

between the two, as well as carrying out her responsibilities as president of the organization. This meant that it was necessary to recruit capable people to assist her in both locations to handle pastoral responsibilities when she was unable to fulfill them and to help her with oversight of the organization. She used both women and men in this capacity.

From the denomination's inception in 1924 until 1936, Robinson was personally involved in planting almost every new local congregation within the Mt. Sinai organization. To do this, she concentrated her ministry on the East Coast. She traveled to small towns such as Fruitland and Easton in Maryland, Smyrna in Delaware, Bridgeton and Salem in New Jersey, and larger cities such as Baltimore, Wilmington, Delaware, and New York. In each of these locations, she conducted revival services, making new converts, and establishing local congregations over which she would place a minister as pastor. Many of these placements were women.[21]

To establish the church in Baltimore, for example, Robinson preached a thirty-day revival at the Goldfield theatre on South Sharpe Street. At the end of the revival, she asked for volunteers to start a new church. She appointed Elder Elmira Jeffries as the pastor of the new start. A testimony by one of her grateful followers in that city described her efforts this way: "Bishop Robinson... was called and commissioned by God to establish a church Baltimore. She along with her group from Philadelphia conducted a thirty-day revival. Bishop Robinson had a vision that many people in the city would be saved."[22]

Testimonies of her tireless involvement in establishing new works abound in the commemorative material. This anecdotal evidence gives insight into the church planting methodology employed by Robinson: "Bishop Robinson came to the town of Fruitland, Maryland in 1923 to conduct a revival. [Later,] Bishop Robinson brought $700 with her to build the church."[23] "In 1924, Bishop Robinson traveled from Philadelphia [to Easton, Maryland]. During this mission, the gallant

149

saints from the city followed Bishop Robinson into Dobson Hall and broke up a dance. This marked the start of the first Christianized group of people."[24]

When Robinson did not establish a congregation herself, she sent others to selected locations specifically for that purpose. Often she sent women, individually or in teams. Sometimes she sent mixed pairs. People who served well in these initial assignments were elevated through the ranks to serve in the leadership of the various auxiliary ministries and governing bodies of the organization. Most of the growth in the organization occurred while Robinson's was actively involved in either starting congregations or appointing people to go into communities and plant congregations.

Besides her seemingly tireless energy in birthing churches, Robinson's captivating personality also played a big role in building up her organization. People were attracted to her as an individual and many came to the church specifically to be under her leadership. Her charismatic attraction was so strong that there are stories of people relocating so they could attend her church and work with her.[25]

In one such story, which recounted an early episode in Robinson's ministry, a woman whom Robinson had befriended while living in Florida as a young woman uprooted her household and followed Robinson and her family to Philadelphia.[26] That woman, Rosa Bell, became a member of Robinson's church and was one of the first officers of the new corporation. She later became a minister and a person of some influence in the Mt. Sinai organization.[27]

Another draw to Robinson's church was her engaging ministry style that involved singing and preaching intermixed as she would come down from the pulpit and walk the aisles of the gathered congregation to be near her people. Her sermons sometimes lasted for two to three hours, and on Sundays she often would preach two or three sermons. Along with being an excellent preacher, Robinson gave

150

a lot of attention to teaching her members. She set aside nights specifically for Bible teaching, and she spent several hours a week studying the Scripture.

Whether she started it or not, Robinson was involved in the ongoing nurture of each congregation and its ministers. She regularly traveled up and down the East Coast to visit each church, to check on the health of the congregation, and to encourage each pastor. She would often stay in a location for several days and preach a revival to help build up the congregation and its finances. When there were problems in a congregation, she either went to see about them or sent a representative—usually a bishop, sometimes an elder.

Another mechanism she used to build up her fledgling congregations was the annual convocation held at the mother church. This was a week of teaching and preaching and recounting what God was doing in the various local congregations. It was also a time for fellowship and a time to promote the specific interests within the organization and collect special offerings to support its various ministries.

Like McPherson and Crawford, Robinson was aware of the potential power of the electronic media for increasing the evangelistic outreach of the church. From the 1930s through the 1940s, Robinson had an hour-long radio broadcast on WNEW in New York City. The broadcast emanated from the Sunday worship services of the headquarters, Bethel Holy Church, in upper Manhattan. Her Sunday messages reached as far as North Carolina. People who heard her on the radio often made a special trip to see the dynamic preacher in action. Several of them stayed to become members.

Despite its eschatological sounding title, the organization's newsletter, The Latter Day Messenger, dealt with a variety of social, ethical, and religious issues. Articles written by Robinson and excerpts from her sermons, testimonials, and praise reports from the various congregations, constituent letters, and other individual contributions showed the breadth of Robinson's concerns as well as the concerns of her congregants. Amid birth announcements or coverage of members' weddings, issues such as racial and economic discrimination, race relations, and women's role in the church stood side by side with doctrinal discussions.

Substantive contributions from constituents included articles such as one from a young woman in Pensacola, Florida, entitled "What a Christian Teacher Can Do for Negro America."[28] It lauded the contribution of Christian teachers to the secular education of African American children, testified to the writer's own experiences as a young teacher, and encouraged readers to consider teaching as a profession.

Other contributions highlighted the gifts of those who used their talents to underscore the founder's views on pertinent issues. An excerpt from a poem, submitted by one of Robinson's women proteges who rose to some prominence within the organization, echoes the founder's sentiments:

> You'll wish you had let women alone
> When they were trying to teach
> You'll be sorry you tried to hold them down
> When God told them to preach...
> Does not the Bible plainly tell you
> Women shall co-ordinate with man?
> The hand that rocks the cradle
> Will rule the world you know...
>
> Some women have the right to sing
> And some the right to teach
> But women, called by Jesus Christ,
> Surely have the right to preach.

Some men will call you anti-Christ
And some would rather die
Than have the Spirit poured out
When women prophesy.[29]

Whether the newsletter was reserved for distribution in Robinson's denomination or if it had a wider distribution among outside supporters is unknown, so a true gauge of its impact on spreading Robinson's views and ministry is not available.

As an astute businesswoman and administrator, Robinson was considered financially successful for a black woman of her time. While there is no estimate of just how much money Robinson received over several years as head of Mt. Sinai, one 1936 article in Crisis magazine referred to her as the "well-to-do Mrs. Robinson."[30] Reportedly she received enough to purchase a luxury car to transport her to her various speaking engagements.[31]

The financial success she and her organization enjoyed came from both her business acuity and the effectiveness of the financial support system set up for the organization she headed. Members of Mt. Sinai were expected to tithe their income to the church, and though most were not wealthy, the high rate of compliance resulted in the organization amassing a relatively substantial amount of money. The proceeds of the tithe became property of the pastor and each pastor paid a tithe of that tithe to the general church—or its leader.[32]

Robinson, however, did not live lavishly at the expense of her organization. Rather, effectively managing the group's financial matters and using her acumen and that of those she selected to handle the business affairs, she was able to acquire substantial funds to purchase several properties, in addition to church buildings, and run several related nonprofit organizations, including a school and a 140-acre farm.

Robinson was generous in using the organization's money to care for the people and congregations under her auspices. Both her house in Philadelphia and her apartment over the sanctuary in New York were described as homes away from home for her followers and were open for members to congregate before, between, and after worship services. Several members lived in her houses for various lengths of time as their need required. During the Depression, the Mt. Sinai organization attempted to minister to the temporal needs of the surrounding communities through h setting up a soup kitchen and other outreach programs at Mt. Olive to address the dire need that was evident. After her death, the Mt. Sinai organization established a nursing home to take care of elderly or indigent members.[33]

Legacy of Piety and Justice

Robinson's ministry style would best be described as nurturing and intimate. She paid attention to each member of the Mt. Sinai organization and was highly visible to her congregation. As she preached, she walked the aisles of the church, breaking into song as she saw fit and calling on people by name to make a point on a given subject. But Robinson's message and ministry were not only focused on saving souls and preparing them for heaven. She was genuinely concerned with the welfare of her congregations and the entire African American community in the here and now.

A portion of the tithes Robinson received provided seed money for planting new churches through a revolving fund that loaned money specifically for the financing of the building of new structures. As congregations repaid loans, moneys were returned to the fund to be available for other new churches. On some occasions, Robinson took substantial offerings with her to the fledgling congregations that she visited on her many evangelistic tours and gave them as grants or loans from the mother church.[34]

Sometime during the 1930s, Robinson purchased a farm in rural Bridgeville, New Jersey. Robinson Farm (as it came to be known) contained a hotel that provided housing and gainful employment for members of the Mt. Sinai organization. It was the social gathering place for the "saints" for special occasions and holidays because (in line with the classical Pentecostal tendency toward separatism) they did not want to attend events with "unsaved" or "worldly" people. The farm also served as the site for annual mass baptism services when people from the smaller Mt. Sinai churches gathered to see dozens of people baptized by Robinson.[35]

In 1944-45, the farm was confiscated by the federal government and used as a prisoner of war camp for German war criminals.[36] Old-timers tell of visiting the farm during those years and being able to see and talk to the German prisoners between eating picnic lunches and playing games.[37] Robinson also funded missionary work in South America.[38] The first mission church was organized in Cuba. Later a congregation was organized in British Guyana.[39]

Robinson was theologically conservative, holding to such doctrines as the inerrancy of scripture, the virgin birth, and a literal heaven and hell. Under her leadership, the Mt Sinai organization adhered to a rigidly pietistic moral code that covered many areas of the individual members' lives. There were restrictions on social activities, dress, and family relations. Members of Mt. Sinai were forbidden to attend secular events such as movies or sporting events. They were to abstain from alcoholic beverages and tobacco products. The restrictions on dress were primarily for women and came about in part from Robinson's early exposure to the Church of God. She was impressed by the plain black and white "uniforms" that the saints wore and adopted this style of dress for the women in her church. Therefore,

155

"black dresses with starched white cuffs and collars... became the outfit that identified early [women] members of the Mt. Sinai Holy Church of America."[40] Men were restricted from wearing neckties or anything but white shirts with their dark suits.[41]

The denomination held rigid sanctions against divorce, and remarriage of divorced persons whose ex-spouses were living was forbidden. The stricture was carried out to such a degree that persons who had previously divorced and remarried before joining Mt Sinai were required to terminate the current marriage—especially if they were involved in ministry. One person to have experienced this stricture was Mary E. Jackson, third presiding bishop of the body. In her early life, she had been married to a man whom she divorced. In later years, having been told by his mother that he was dead, Jackson married a member of Mt Sinai who was also a minister. Afterward, she found out that her first husband was still living. Subsequently, she and her new husband decided to live separately, though they never divorced and remained friends.[42]

Despite holding conservative views of personal piety, Robinson was socially progressive in several ways. She was not only interested in providing spiritual leadership for her congregations (that is, in helping them live holy lives in preparation for the hereafter); she also attempted to provide moral leadership as well (helping them live more productive and free lives in this present world). To bring this about, Robinson was not afraid to take unpopular stands on controversial issues; she therefore was not without controversy within the circle of people acquainted with her. One organization that knew of her and kept up with her activities was the United States government-the Federal Bureau of Investigation.

A series of factors kept Robinson under the Federal Bureau of Investigation (FBI) surveillance in the 1930s and 1940s. First, her congregation was racially mixed at a time when segregation, even in the

North, was at its height. Among the white members of her congregation was her secretary, a German woman, married to an Italian man. During the Second World War, they were suspected of sympathizing with the enemy-which brought the congregation under suspicion of harboring enemy sympathizers.[43]

During the war, Robinson was an outspoken pacifist, as were many African American Pentecostals of that day. Members of Mount Sinai were permitted to serve in the armed forces, but only as conscientious objectors. She used her radio broadcast to take stands on her moral convictions, including her stance against supporting the war effort. This action brought severe consequences from the federal government. Twice in 1942, she was placed on the FBI list of suspected agitators for remarks she allegedly made supporting Japanese victories during the early war years Whether or not Robinson made the alleged remarks is under contention; her name was later dropped from the FBI list.[44]

Another example of Robinson's moral courage and ability to tackle issues beyond the specific spiritual needs of her constituency is an article she wrote for The Latter Day Messenger entitled "The Economic Persecution."[45] In it, Robinson prominently attacked racial discrimination in America and compared the lynching of blacks in the southern United States with the persecution of Christians under pagan (sic) emperors of the early centuries.[46] She also attacked the hypocrisy of the southern white church for not taking a stand against the hideous occurrences she graphically depicts or standing against racism in general:

> Our people in certain southern states are killed, their bodies dismembered and thrown to vultures. This, of course[,] is a common occurrence, and unfortunately where "Christianity" is more prevalent than any part of our

157

union. For in this section of the country, laws are made to uphold Christianity in their states, and to prevent any teachings in their institutions of learning that tends to distort, minimize, or otherwise change the principle of the doctrine of Christianity as taught in the Bible.

... It is written in their laws concerning modernism or any other doctrine hostile to the teachings of Jesus "that if anyone is found guilty of teaching doctrine contrary to Christianity in any [state] supported school [that person] shall be punished to the extent of the law." But these same people, in the same sections will toss their own laws to the four winds and trample under feet the laws of Christianity and utterly ignore the words of the sacred "Book" they pretend to love so dearly, and esteem so highly...

...The relationship that exists between Gentile and Jew, as well as Ethiopians[,] is inseparable and unquestionably established. So let us Saints pray that the Constantine of our day sends a letter to the modern pagans in the polluted southland in the form of "Anti-Lynching" legislation that is now pending in Congress. We can overcome and we will overcome, right here in this present world, the persecution we ar[e] made to suffer by our unjust brethren. It is written, the Ethiopians shall stretch forth their hands in righteousness to God, and by the help of God and the agencies He has so gloriously provided, we shall overcome.[47]

Although Robinson probably went to school only to fourth grade, she exhibited a high level of intelligence as well as evidence of being well-read and having a genuine appreciation for learning. In her . sermons and writings, she referred to a variety of sources beyond the Bible. References in "The Economic Persecution" show evidence that Robinson read, appreciated, and quoted from opinion polls, ancient history, and Shakespeare, among other sources.[48]

This appreciation for learning was, in part, responsible for her decision to establish a fully accredited school serving elementary through high school students in the city of Philadelphia. Located next to Mt. Olive, it had boarding facilities and a curriculum that covered a wide range of subjects, including math, science, art, home economics, and, of course, religious studies.

The school operated in the 1930s. The leadership of the school (including superintendent Robinson) prided itself on having high academic standards. It employed only certified teachers and encouraged them to involve themselves in continuing education enrichment courses during the summer. Its recruiting brochure boasted that "any pupil, having finished the elementary and high school course of Mt. Sinai Holiness School, will be eligible to enter college, and their certificate will be recognized by any good Standard School."[49]

In 1944, when she was only fifty-two, and two years before the end of her life, Robinson began to feel that she should prepare for the future of the denomination after her death. In that same year, she had a near-death encounter that she would later describe as a "heavenly experience of death." When she recovered, she gave this testimony from the pulpit of the mother church in Philadelphia:

I used to sing, "I'll Fly Away," but it wasn't time or the will of God for me to fly away..., instead I just went to sleep. The Lord took me out of this body for three hours, the Angels were all around me ready to appoint me a place when I recognized the sound of a familiar voice and the more I

159

listened, the closer the voice came to me. When I opened my eyes I was back in this world and Elder James Bell was praying. His prayer had reached heaven and God sent me back.[50]

As she often did, Robinson made plans for an extended trip in which she would visit each of the existing Mt Sinai congregations. As she was accustomed to, she was going to encourage each pastor, check on the congregation's health, and set in order any matters that she found to be out of place. She was in the process of carrying out this trip, having gone to Jacksonville and Winter Haven, Florida, when she died suddenly in Winter Haven on April 20, 1946, at the age of fifty-four.

At the time of her death, Robinson had led Mt. Sinai for twenty-two years. In that time, she built a denomination of eighty-four churches, stretching from New England to Florida.[51] At least one schism occurred in Mt. Sinai's early when dissenters, dissatisfied with Robinson's decision to relax a ban on men wearing neckties, pulled out to form Glorious Mt. Sinai Holy Church. Generally, however, the Mt. Sinai organization stayed intact. Individual congregations left from time to time, and a few additional congregations were added.

A more amicable break occurred in 1926, when Eva Lambert withdrew to establish Saint Mark's Holy Gospel Church of America Inc. Lambert had worked very closely with Robinson and with her blessing, moved to New York where she held tent meetings that drew a following large enough to establish the congregation that would be the beginning of Saint Mark's in Brooklyn. For the next thirteen years, several churches came under Lambert's leadership as she remained in fellowship with Robinson's group. In 1939, she was consecrated as a bishop with Robinson's blessing.[52]

Women's Ministry and Leadership

Acting on what she felt was a direct mandate from God, Robinson set out to deliver women from what she saw as the bondage of male domination within her denomination-the United Holy Church of America-and bring them to a place of freedom and equality within her newly formed Mt. Sinai Holy Church of America, Inc. From the outset, Robinson acted strategically to ensure that women were an integral part of the ministry and leadership both in the local congregations that she pastored and throughout the Mt. Sinai Holy Church of America, Inc., organization.

Within her local congregation, Mt. Olive, Robinson instituted specific measures to ensure that women were provided opportunities for ministry and leadership.[53] She set up Monday night as "Women Preacher's Night"—a time specifically for women to preach and sharpen their preaching skills. In these sessions, she observed their style, content, strengths, and weaknesses. Following the sessions, she critiqued and instructed them. She discerned which women were specifically gifted for the preaching ministry. Women as well as men were selected to fill the church's ministries. They served as Sunday school teachers, ushers, and deacons, all the while being trained and developing skills for increasingly more important leadership roles. Robinson selected women from the congregation and enlisted them to assist with her personal needs. As they served as her housekeeper, nurse, driver, or reader, she invested herself in nurturing and preparing them for key leadership roles in these congregations and in the broader body.

Robinson set up a semi-episcopal church government with a parallel system of administrative government for the legal organization and ecclesiastical government for the church.[54] With one major change, this form of government remains in place within the Mt. Sinai organization to the present time. At the top of the structure is the

161

president of the organization, who is the presiding bishop. The presiding bishop is supported by corporate officers (two vice presidents, two secretaries, a treasurer, and two administrators). During Robinson's lifetime, there were no other bishops and the denomination was not divided into jurisdictions. Robinson had oversight of all of the churches.[55] After Robinson's death, however, the denomination put additional bishops in place with either jurisdictional (specified regions) or administrative (specific functions) responsibilities. Together, they form a board of bishops. Elders are the next lower ecclesiastical level, some of whom preside over smaller jurisdictional areas under a bishop. A board of presbyters is made up of jurisdictional bishops and presiding elders. The president—who is also the presiding bishop and chairman of the organization-serves under a board of directors. Other ecclesiastical heads serve in parallel positions as officers and directors of the organization.

The entry level of ministry within Mt. Sinai is the licensed minister. After faithfully serving for a period, a person can be ordained an elder. From the ranks of elder, bishops are consecrated. The functional ministry of the church falls into two categories pastors and evangelists.

Pastors are appointed from the ranks of ministers, elders, or bishops. Evangelists travel from congregation to congregation; they preach for special services such as revivals, church anniversaries, and women's or men's days. Additionally, some deacons are responsible for taking care of the material needs of the congregation.[56]

From the beginning, Robinson licensed and ordained women as well as men to the ministry, and the majority of the ministers she ordained in her first ordination service were women.[57] She ordained women as elders and bishops (not just as ministers), placed them in pastorates, and appointed them to positions of leadership and authority.[58] In the first church established under the newly signed charter in Burgaw, North Carolina, the first pastor Robinson appointed

162

in her fledgling organization was a woman, Melinda Cousins.[59] The first officers of the organization were four women-Robinson as president, Elmira Jeffries as vice president, Mary Jackson as secretary, and Rosa Bell as treasurer. Six of the nine members of the organization's first board of elders were female.[60] The trend of maintaining women in a substantial portion of these leadership roles continues until the present time.

Under Robinson's leadership, Mt. Sinai existed as a female-led— but not female-dominated—organization. Robinson equally enlisted both men and women to work in every aspect of ministry. Men and women were credentialed at every level of ministry and served on boards and committees. In the local congregation, for example, along with the women's night, Robinson instituted a preacher's night for men on Wednesday, giving equal opportunity for fledging young men to sharpen their preaching skills and receive her encouragement and nurture.

As Fauset characterizes the male/female dynamic at Mt. Sinai in his seminal work on the organization, it "is distinctive... in the extent and degree of female participation. Many of the elders are women, as also are a large number of preachers; there are, however, many men in official places."[61] Robinson selected women and men who were in some ways more capable than she was. She was not intimidated by their abilities, but employed them to build her organization to be the largest single African American denomination led by a woman. Somehow she inspired their loyalty and fostered a model of women and men working together harmoniously in positions of leadership for the common cause of the gospel.

By the time of her death, the pattern of women's leadership in Mt. Sinai had been set, for Robinson had inculcated the ideology of equality into her preaching and teaching and modeled it in appointments to church staffs, pastorates, and other leadership positions. The ideology

163

of gender equality had been ingrained into the souls and psyches of her followers so that the next generation of leadership reflected those principles for which Robinson had so tirelessly worked. An indication of how well Robinson's efforts fared in the next generation is the assessment made by one of Mt Sinai's leading current women bishops at the end of the twentieth century. In an article in a nationally circulated magazine geared to the Pentecostal and charismatic community, Bishop Barbara Amos insisted that, "The gender issue is nonexistent in Mount Sinai because every position in the local and national church is open equally to men and women."[62]

The success of Robinson's efforts is reflected in the caliber of women's leadership that existed within the Mt. Sinai organization during her lifetime and following her death. The three women who were to become the denomination's next presiding bishops exemplify how she prepared and empowered women to move into the highest levels of leadership. All three were close to Robinson, served her in some personal capacity, benefited from her mentoring, and served in increasingly important leadership roles in local congregations and the broader church.

The second presiding bishop and president, Elmira Jeffries, served from 1946 to 1964. Jeffries assumed the leadership of Mt. Sinai Holy Church directly after Robinson's death.[63] She had been one of the people to accompany Robinson when she left the United Holy Church and was a charter member of the new organization as well as a charter member of its board.

Jeffries began her ministry in the early days of Mt Sinai by leading the Tuesday noonday tarry service at Robinson's Mt Olive congregation. She served as pastor of several Mt Sinai congregations, primarily in large urban areas, as well as in several positions of increasingly important leadership. Before assuming the position of presiding bishop, Jeffries had served as vice president of the denomination under Robinson.[64]

When Robinson died, eighty-eight-year-old Mary Jackson was elected as vice president. A charter member of Robinson's first congregation in the new denomination, she succeeded Jeffries as third presiding bishop and president, serving for fourteen years until her death at age 102.[65] She had served under Robinson as the secretary of the denomination.[66] Previous to that, she had served as Robinson's reader; because Jackson had more formal education, Robinson called on her to read scriptural texts and books to her, explaining some of the larger words that Robinson did not understand. Jackson's ministry at Mt. Olive began by teaching the preacher's class and assisting Robinson with financial matters. She later served as presiding elder of the Southern District as well as of Mt. Olive, the mother church, and pastored congregations in New Jersey and Delaware. She retired from the active pastorate of Mt. Olive at age one hundred.[67]

At Jackson's death, Amy Bell Stevens was elected presiding bishop and president at age seventy-one and served until her death in 2000 at age eighty-eight.[68] Stevens attended Sunday school at Mt. Sinai after her family moved to Philadelphia when she was twelve. As a young woman, she ushered and taught Sunday school. After completing high school, she attended business school, then nursing school. She entered ministry at age twenty-three, pastoring in Hurlock, Maryland, for six months before being tapped as Robinson's personal nurse. In a move that might seem incomprehensible, Stevens relinquished her pastorate and came back to Philadelphia to serve in what some would consider a menial position. But in that position, she lived and traveled with Robinson and became intimately acquainted with her. In the hours they spent together, Stevens received special mentoring and nurturing that Robinson was noted for giving to the women around her while at the same time being groomed for greater leadership positions.

Leaving Philadelphia, Stevens pastored congregations in Mt. Holly, New Jersey, and Wilmington, Delaware, finally returning to Mt. Olive, where she served until her death. She held several increasingly important leadership positions beginning with her first position as secretary of the ministers' board at age twenty-three. She also served as secretary of the board of directors, presiding elder of the Pennsylvania/New Jersey Diocese, and vice president.

The personal service each of these women provided Robinson in some non-ministerial capacity speaks to the role mentoring played in Robinson's relationship with them. But whether Robinson initially identified them as persons worthy of extra attention or whether they aggressively sought out such attention is not known.

In assessing Robinson's theological stand on women's ministry and leadership, we can call on the few public statements she is known to have made about the issue. Published doctrinal statements from Mt. Sinai Holy Church cover a full range of Christian beliefs and practical living but, surprisingly, give little attention to women's role in ministry and church leadership.

Of the four Pentecostal women pioneers who are the subjects of this book—Tate, Crawford, McPherson, and Robinson-Robinson certainly went furthest in delineating any theological premise for the equal treatment of women in the church. However, one shortcoming is that she never took steps to ensure that this premise would be codified for future generations of church members, women ministers, and historians. Remnants of her ideology do remain, and from them, one forms a picture of a woman who believed in the equality of all before God and the need for women to take a rightful place beside men in the leadership of the church. Harold Dean Trulear describes Robinson's "hermeneutic" as involving a biblical defense of women in a movement that takes the written Word of God seriously while tackling the controversial passages that seem to indicate God's

166

prohibition against women preachers. Robinson's defense of women's leadership and claim for their full clergy rights are based on four pivotal biblical ideas: (1) the creation narrative in Genesis I and 2, (2) the example of Mary, mother of Jesus, (3) the story of the women who first told of Jesus' resurrection, and (4) the equality of male and female in the body of Christ.[69]

In the first instance, Trulear interprets Robinson as distinguishing between the creation and formation of humankind; seeing in this distinction God's creative intention of equality between the sexes. For him, Robinson reads Genesis 1 and 2 as chronological history. For her, in Genesis 1, God created male and female in his image. It is as this being, with created male and female essence, that Adam is given dominion over all the earth. Therefore, dominion and leadership belong to both male and female. In Genesis 2, God subsequently formed Adam and Eve as separate, gender-distinct beings, who had already been created.[70] They did not give up equality at this point. He reports one of Robinson's ministers as characterizing the essence of her understanding of equality in creation this way: "Her name really is Eve Adam, for she shares in his being, dominion, and position of privilege with God, based on her creation in Genesis 1."[71]

Trulear posits that Robinson, in looking at Mary, the mother of Jesus, saw a model of the significant role women played in the salvation story. Her often quoted retort, "If Mary can carry the Word of God in her womb, why can't I carry the Word of God on my lips?"[72] speaks of the import she attached to Mary as a model of the leadership role available to any woman God chooses to use.

For Robinson, the story of the women disciples' announcing news of the resurrection meant that they were the first preachers in the newly formed church. She underscored their deeds as the foundation of the New Testament Church and upheld its importance for her contemporaries called to ministry. According to Trulear, at every

Easter Sunday sunrise service Bishop Robinson would lead her congregation in singing a chorus that spoke of the importance she gave to these women:

Didn't those women run, Didn't those women run?
They ran the good news to spread. The angel told them to go.
For Jesus had gone on before. He is risen just as he said.[73]

The Pauline proclamation that "there is neither male nor female [in Christ]" (Gal. 3:28) provided the final premise for a claim for equality of women. Though some would claim that the statement does not deal with ministry or leadership, but rather with one's relationship with Christ, Robinson saw it as encompassing both arenas. For her, this equality, reiterated in the redemption brought to us by Christ, reflected the equality intended in creation.[74] This intended equality included the capacity to be and work in quality relations with each other. It was Christ's redemptive act that restored the equal status of men and women before God that was lost in the fall.

Legacy for Women

Robinson's heavy emphasis on the equality of women in ministry bore much fruit during the early years of Mt. Sinai. Women were given what Trulear refers to as "full clerical and episcopal rights that provided an opportunity to use and develop their unique gifts at every level of the organization during her lifetime."[75] Again, Robinson worked to ensure that the ethos of equality ran throughout her organization. Because of her efforts, women continue to play an integral part in the ministry of Mt. Sinai more than fifty years after her death.

The overall impact of Robinson's efforts on Pentecostalism, her community, and that world was restricted by the small size of the Mt. Sinai Holy Church. In the first twenty years of its existence, the

168

denomination grew by an average of four new congregations a year, so that by the time of Robinson's death in 1944, eighty-four congregations had been birthed. At its height, in 1988, forty-four years after her death, the organization had grown to 154 congregations. primarily along the East Coast, 1996, this number was down to 102, with approximately ten thousand members. One congregation was in Cuba, seven house churches in India, and two in Guyana, South America.[76] In 2000, the denomination had decreased to 114 congregations, a net loss of 30 congregations from the 1988 figures.[77]

Its constituency is predominantly African American, and in comparison to its sister bodies such as the Church of God in Christ, its parent United Holy Church, and the Fire Baptized Holiness Church, for example, the body remains large unknown outside of that community of Pentecostals and the growth that Mt. Sinai experienced under Robinson was never again realized.

Though proponents tout her impact on the role of women in the Pentecostal movement as major, Robinson and her organization have been largely ignored by those outside her immediate sphere. For example, in *Daughters of Thunder*, Betty Collier-Thomas says that Robinson's "impact on her time and black religion were singular."[78] Yet, in fact, she appears to have had little impact on her time or on black religion; to have been largely forgotten after her death. Still, Remnants of information about her work have been barely kept alive by a small group of followers within the Mt. Sinai organization and individual scholars of African American religion such as Trulear.

Collier-Thomas' assertion that Robinson is well known to Pentecostal-Holiness advocates is not completely supportable. Certainly, several anthologies of women's or African American biographies include short articles on Robinson, and several encyclopedic works on African American religion give Mt. Sinai Holy Church of America a brief discussion. Yet, most Pentecostal scholarship completely ignores her, or give her passing notice or a singular notation related to women as leaders.

Such mitigating factors reduce the impact of Robinson's efforts to improve women's situation in the Pentecostal movement both during her lifetime and after her death. Yet women continued to be involved in ministry within the Mt. Sinai organization, and the top leadership person remained a woman for seventy-five years. Since its inception until Bishop Stevens' death in 2000, the leadership of the denomination never passed out of the hands of women. Up to that time, all four of the denomination's presiding bishops had been women. At Stevens' death, leadership passed into the hands of the first man, Bishop Joseph Bell.

The rate of women's participation in top leadership positions has continued to decline from the time of Robinson's death until the present. There remain large numbers of women in ministry, but the proportion of women pastors and women with governing and oversight responsibilities continues to slowly, but steadily, fall. Of the 160 ordained ministers[79] who were part of the organization in 1996, 125 (more than three-fourths) were women.[80] However, only forty-five of the 102 pastors were women, and only eight of the nineteen bishops.[81]

In the fifty-six years from Bishop Robinson's death until 2000, the decline in the number of women in the pastorate has continually accelerated. In the first twenty-six years, there was only a 9 percent decrease. However, in the succeeding twenty-four years, the rate of decrease almost doubled to 16 percent. Apparently generations less familiar with Robinson are also less familiar with ideals that were core to her ministry. Certainly, these ideals are less important than they once were. More importantly, however, most current women bishops are older and came into the church and rose in rank during or shortly after Robinson's lifetime. These women are revered for their contributions,

170

but most are no longer able to contribute viable input to Mt. Sinai's governance. The male bishops tend to be younger and more recently elected. They tend to be the decision-makers—and are therefore the real leadership of the Mt. Sinai organization. Over the years, a pattern of preference for male leadership at the higher levels of authority has, clearly, been developing within Mt. Sinai. As early as 1980, considerably less than one-half of leaders were women, and by 2000, only one-third of Mt. Sinai bishops were women.

Conclusion

Because of her giftedness for ministry-her ability to preach, teach, sing, and pray with the "anointing"—Robinson's position in the United Holy Church was secure. She had personal liberty and was highly esteemed. Had she remained in that body, she might have been singled out as an example of an "exceptional" woman whose "gifts" would make room for her being elevated to increasingly higher levels of leadership. Because of limitations on other women in that body, however, she might have stood alone at those levels. This was simply not sufficient for her. Robinson did not see herself as a particularly exceptional woman. Instead, she saw all women who were called of God as qualified and capable of moving into whatever position of leadership God had ordained for them. She saw the restrictions placed upon her sisters as unwarranted and her mission as more than securing her own individual position and recognition.

Robinson did not see herself adding anything unique to Pentecostal theology that made her organization stand out against existing bodies. She had been nurtured in two mainstream Pentecostal bodies-the Church of God and the United Holy Church. She felt at home with the core of classical Pentecostal belief and never attempted to promulgate any new doctrine outside that of mainstream Holiness-Pentecostalism. Rather, driven by a vision from God of liberating

171

women from hierarchical strictures of existing Pentecostal denominations, she set out to change the status of women's leadership in the African American Pentecostal church culture. She attempted to do this by creating a denomination in which women were given complete freedom to use their God-given gifts and serve in every capacity of ministry without limitation.

This gifted woman did not promote her own ministry, though she was highly respected within the United Holy Church. But the restrictions on the role of women in that body—the rescission of the right to the public ordination of women, the failure to place women as pastors in viable congregations, and the limitations on the leadership role of women—was the catalyst for forming the Mt. Sinai Holy Church of America, Inc. There is no evidence that Robinson ever attempted to reform the United Holy Church on its position on women's leadership—to change the minds of denominational leaders or rally women to protest for their rights within that body. She did not attempt to bring about social justice within the denomination. Instead, she attempted to create a new organization that would model the social justice she desired. Within this new body, she sought to identify, train, nurture, place, and promote women—and men—whom she felt exemplified spiritual traits that suited them for ministerial leadership. At the same time, she preached a message of holiness patterned after the organizations with which she had previously been affiliated.

The name "Mt. Sinai" stands as a prophetic witness to a visionary woman's desire to bring about a specific deliverance. Just as Moses was called to deliver Israel, Robinson sensed a call to deliver the women of the United Holy Church. Like Moses, Robinson saw no real value in attempting to win small victories for women within the United Holy Church. Instead, she took the radical step of seeking to bring them to a whole new "land of freedom" where all barriers and restrictions for ministry and leadership based on gender had been destroyed.

Conclusion

As the early, limited openness to women's leadership in the classical Pentecostal movement gave way to tighter restrictions and traditional ideas about gender and place, four seemingly ordinary women—Florence Louise Crawford, Mary Magdalena Lewis Tate, Aimee Semple McPherson, and Ida Bell Robinson-individually challenged limitation of their God-given liberty to preach the gospel. They sought not only freedom to preach, but full clergy rights-liberty to set up their congregations as they saw fit, oversee those congregations, and direct the work of other ministers whom they had nurtured in the faith. In gaining her liberty, each left standing a denominational legacy of successful women's leadership.

For nearly one hundred years, however, their collective contribution to the classical Pentecostal view of women remained unappreciated and their stories, largely, untold. McPherson's name generally brings some recognition, mostly for her dramatic pulpit antics and the questionable circumstances of her life. Florence Crawford is recognized only among avid students of early Pentecostalism. The names Mary Magdalena Tate and Ida Robinson hold little name recognition, even within African American Pentecostalism of which they are a part. Yet a serious exploration of these women's lives and ministries evokes a portrait of exceptional accomplishments that can serve as a model for generations of Christian women with the courage to learn from them.

Their narratives repeatedly show a powerful sense of call and an awareness that the empowerment of the Holy Spirit fit them to accomplish something extraordinary for God. Although their perceptions of vocation differed greatly, in pursuing that call each acted to build a spiritual organization in which they—and their sisters—

175

would be free to pursue their divinely called vocations without limitation. Crawford felt called to maintain a standard of holiness and rally spiritual resources against the laxity she saw encroaching on the nascent movement. Tate saw her vocation as reviving true holiness and recreating the New Testament Church in which, significantly, women were to equally share leadership with men. Robinson was specifically summoned to build an organization in which women would play a prominent role, loosed from restrictions imposed by a hierarchical denominational structure. McPherson saw her vocation as an evangelist; she felt called simply to win as many souls to faith in Christ as possible and minister a holistic gospel that included a strong emphasis on divine healing. In the end, the sheer strength of these calls enabled these four women to work with singleness of purpose to accomplish what they saw as their God-ordained missions. Rather than try to persuade with rhetoric or biblical arguments, they allowed their accomplishments to speak for the appropriateness of women's leadership.

More than a ceremonial mantle, the title of bishop that Tate and Robinson wore signified their identified leadership and spoke of the authority vested in them as head of their respective denominations.[1] While Crawford and McPherson respectively bore simpler titles— "mother" and "sister"—they both took their authority within their young organizations equally seriously. Each woman acted as a general overseer, appointing key persons within her respective organization, and setting its doctrinal and spiritual agenda during her lifetime, while providing a legacy for generations to come.

As astute administrators, these women involved themselves in their organizations' fiscal and administrative oversight, which, in each case, grew to encompass substantial property worth millions of dollars and included educational and social services and auxiliary facilities, as well as substantial houses of worship. Skillful fiscal management allowed them to defy the storefront stereotype often attached to female Pentecostal ministers, and instead to acquire or build and fill substantial edifices with seating capacities in the hundreds and thousands.

Crawford not only acquired property for a sanctuary but built a headquarters with a camp meeting facility on several acres of real estate within the city of Portland, Oregon. McPherson's five-thousand-seat Angeles Temple opened debt-free. One of the several buildings Robinson used to house Mt. Olive, the mother church of Mt. Sinai, was a 2,500-seat edifice that was the first holiness church on Philadelphia's main east-west thoroughfare. Tate's local churches were generally housed in traditional church buildings or substantially renovated facilities, rather than simple storefronts.

Women's Ministry and Leadership

Pentecostalism has often been characterized as other-worldly and accommodationist, a claim that is most true in its early period; however, a purely accommodationist position does not fit any of these women. None of them contented themselves with the status quo. Neither did they resign themselves to traditional roles they saw as unbiblical. The denominations that Crawford, Tate, Robinson, and McPherson crafted also defy the accommodationist label-in part, because their ministries were concerned about the material, temporal well-being of constituents as much as their spiritual, eternal well-being and demonstrated that concern in tangible steps undertaken to ensure that their flocks and communities received the sustenance they needed. Rescue work, soup kitchens, housing, and schools were as much a part of their ministries as were revival-style worship and faith healing.

While not attempting to change women's status for the entire Pentecostal movement, they understood that they could change their own situation and proceeded to do so. They never internalized the

177

imposed perception of women's limitations and allowed no limits on themselves. So neither could they be viewed as reformist, because they never fully accepted the values of the gender-biased structures around them. They did not buy into prevailing notions that women's ministry had to be complementary or that women were somehow less suited for leadership. Further, they did not attempt to change women's expectations to fit into the existing denominational structure, for this would have meant lowering those expectations to the point that women could largely serve only in support roles.

Earlier biblical feminists attempted to influence structures through strategic and radical activism. By holding meetings, launching petition drives, lobbying, public speaking, and nonviolent resistance, women in the suffrage movement and the women's rights movement worked deliberately to create a place for themselves within the larger society. But Crawford, Tate, McPherson, and Robinson were not radical activists. None of them directly confronted the male leadership within classical Pentecostalism, demanding a broader place for women and their leadership. They never challenged existing power structures to weaken or eliminate the male stranglehold on Pentecostal leadership. Such tactics would have seemed inappropriate in a spiritual milieu in which corporal intervention was itself deemed carnal.[2] They would have dismissed any description of themselves as feminists or any language demanding "equal rights" in the church. Such talk would have been deemed sinful.

They did not attempt to change the existing Pentecostal denominations so that these bodies would be more accepting of women. They did not attempt to bring about a political coup to topple the male leadership and replace it with women. Unlike their contemporaries in the women's suffrage movement and the women's rights movement, they did not organize politically, they held no boycotts, and they infiltrated no ecclesial meetings to interrupt them with loud protest and placards. Nor did they withhold financial support, march, or hold prayer vigils.

Instead, each attempted to show a different way to be a church in which spiritual giftedness and commitment replaced maleness as criteria for ministry and leadership. Each worked to create places for herself where she would be unhampered by gender bias. All four first established congregations, then denominations, that modeled women freely fulfilling their leadership potential without regard to artificial limitations imposed by a male hierarchy. But their churches also had little influence on their sister denominations, which continued to operate—and even today, still operate-within a male-dominated hierarchy.

These were women from common working-class backgrounds, though Crawford and McPherson were probably somewhat better off than either Tate's or Robinson's upbringings allowed them to be. Certainly, cultural influences and social location played a role in the development of each woman's denomination, for within American society, race has always been a factor in assessing the relative worth of individual contributions in any arena. The church and religious world is no exception. The role of race in working out the situations of Crawford, Tate, McPherson, and Robinson is most evident in two areas: their perception of women's role in the white vs. black societies and the disparity in the number of people their ministries touched and influenced. But this is not the focus of this study; suffice it to say that within the highly segregated environment that characterized early twentieth-century America, Tate and Robinson were aware of the racial discrimination that blacks received and, to some extent, this awareness guided the type of ministry they provided to their constituencies. This awareness led both women to set up social outreach and social justice components such as schools to expressly address the inferior education of their African American constituents. It was also this awareness that

179

caused them to address racial issues as much as or more than gender issues in the limited writing that they did.

What might these women have accomplished had they individually taken a radical activist stance to challenge the early Pentecostal presuppositions that upheld the limited status of women? More importantly, what might they have collectively accomplished had time and circumstances allowed them to corporately attack gender bias? Unfortunately, these questions remain unanswered; these women's paths never crossed, for a variety of reasons. One of them was, certainly, the racial climate of the period that would have kept Crawford and McPherson in separate circles from Tate and Robinson. While integrated worship events were sometimes held, especially in the large evangelistic services and revivals that these women used as vehicles for ministry, the Holiness and Pentecostal movements showed some of the same patterns of racial segregation as did the larger society.[3] Second, though they each traveled extensively, Crawford and McPherson were based on the West Coast; Tate and Robinson were based on the East Coast, Tate primarily in the rural South and Robinson primarily in the cities and rural areas of the Mid-Atlantic states. Additionally, Crawford and Tate's ministries preceded that of the other two women by several years. It· was only six years after McPherson's Angelus Temple was opened and Robinson's Mt. Sinai Holy Church of America came into being that Tate died. Crawford died only five years later.

Encouraging Women's Ongoing Leadership

For a variety of reasons, Crawford, Tate, McPherson, and Robinson were not explicitly engaged in developing theologies to encourage the leadership of women. Yet what they did in setting up their respective denominations implicitly encouraged women's leadership. They were not concerned with creating an ongoing legacy

180

because they genuinely expected that Jesus would return shortly. If he was not to come in their lifetime, they reasoned they surely were ushering in the generation in which his return would take place. So they saw their responsibility as primarily reaching lost souls. Their most enduring legacy to women is the relatively strong institutions they left behind. Today, even while those institutions are largely led by men, evidence of the imprint of these women remains engrafted within their very fabric.

McPherson's most important contribution to the continued leadership of women was establishing L.I.FE. Bible colleges in the United States and Canada and opening them to women as a means of training for the ministry. She sent women out-sometimes as individuals, but often as members of husband and wife teams-to plant and nurture new congregations. She also elevated a small number of women to secondary places of authority within the Foursquare denomination. The highest places of authority, however, were generally held by men.

Both Tate and Robinson undertook specific steps to ensure that women played significant roles in their ministry during their lifetimes and that they would play an ongoing role after their demise. Each woman selected and trained other women to follow in their footsteps. They sought out women-as well as men-in whom they saw the gifts of preaching, teaching, and administration-the pastoral gifts-and they nurtured them, entrusted them with increasingly more responsibility, and groomed them to move into increasingly higher levels of leadership. They placed these women in strategic places—as pastors, corporate officers, presiding elders, and bishops.

Additionally, Tate incorporated the simple language of gender equality into her doctrinal statement by explicitly stating that God equally called men and women to ministry. She sent men and women out in teams to work together from the lowest role of church planter

181

to higher positions of co-pastors and co-elders. In this move, she was modeling the idea of equality and cooperation between the sexes in ministry. Even though many of the top leaders in the Church of the Living God, the Pillar and Ground of the Truth, Inc., were related to Tate by blood or marriage, these men and women worked side by side.

Robinson's group was the only one of the four denominations established specifically to encourage women to move into ministerial leadership. Robinson not only included the language of equality into Mt. Sinai's doctrinal statement; she also incorporated regular opportunities for women to hone their preaching craft within the structure of her church calendar. She selected women to work intimately with her in roles that, at first glance, would appear to be subservient, traditional roles for women. But she regularly deployed these women for every type of ministry within Mt. Sinai, without denigrating the contribution of men in any way.

In this way, the men and women in the Mt. Sinai Holy Church became accustomed to working beside each other in leadership positions. As they grew used to such equal working relations, the ethos of gender equality was infused into the fabric of the Mt. Sinai organization in such a way that after her death, women served at the helm of Mt. Sinai for sixty years, through three changes in administration. Mt. Sinai, although currently presided over by a man, still provided the greatest opportunity for women's leadership among Pentecostal bodies. But a steady pattern of decline and somewhat isolationist tendencies has meant that the denomination has had little impact on the broader Pentecostal movement.

Robinson's major flaw was her failure to perceive the historical importance of what she was attempting to do. Because of that, she failed to provide other than primarily oral instruction and nurturing to the women who surrounded her. The legacy of inclusiveness and empowerment of women and the import of what she was doing went largely undisclosed beyond the Mt. Sinai community for several decades. Additionally, as the generations that personally knew her continue to die out, the inclusive ethos is beginning to be diluted and is being gradually replaced by a male-dominated leadership.

These four women did not understand that what they were doing was making a difference in the ministries of women beyond their denomination. With all they did to directly, or indirectly, enlarge a place for women's leadership within their lifetimes, they sought no systemic change in the larger Pentecostal movement or improvement in the situation of the bulk of Pentecostal women, who would choose to remain in existing bodies for generations to come. There were several reasons for this.

Again, they shared the Pentecostal understanding that Jesus was soon to return and reserved their energies for training workers to win as many souls as possible. Like most adherents and leaders of the early Pentecostal movement, they saw themselves as living in a time of crisis—during the end-time revival just before Christ's return, when God was "pour[ing] out [the]Spirit on all flesh" Joel 2:28; Acts 2:16-18). For them, the luxury of reflection and writing about issues not central to the salvation of souls for Christ's coming could not be afforded.

Second, they were singularly focused on achieving their own vocational goals-as they felt called by God to achieve. And though, of the four, Robinson's vocational goals were most clearly aligned with making a place for women's leadership to flourish, even her ministry focused on creating a new place, not opening up existing structures.

Last, these women were not theologians, trained to think systematically about issues such as gender bias. They could recognize elements of such bias that hindered their own vocational call and worked to lessen the import of that bias on their own ministry and, resultantly, on the ministries of the men and women who worked with

183

them. When, for example, Robinson learned that her organization would no longer publicly ordain women, she might have made any one of a number of responses, including strategically approaching the leadership to change their minds. Or she might have rallied her sisters to launch a radical protest to force the denomination to recant that position. Either of these actions may have had some success in bringing about a degree of change in the United Holy Church's stance on women's leadership. Instead, Robinson chose to leave the United Holy Church to form a liberating place for women. In doing so, she left her parent denomination largely unchanged regarding women's leadership. Women are only now beginning to enjoy full clergy rights within the United Holy Church. By the early twenty-first century, three women had risen to the position of bishop in that denomination.

Yet when examined closely, Crawford, Tate, McPherson, and Robinson's individual and collective contributions have implications beyond their denominations. For these were women of spoken word and action-not written word. For them, this spoken word was the gospel of salvation through Jesus Christ, not a theological tome regarding the equality and inclusiveness of women in the life, ministry, and leadership of the church. They did not refute such theology or deny its importance, but it was not their focus.

Theirs was a lived theology of inclusiveness portrayed in their actions. Rather than work to radically change the male-dominated system of early classical Pentecostalism and in doing so possibly break the fellowship of that community, they stepped out and formed sister denominations that shared the common Pentecostal faith and ethos, but added-intentionally or not-the element of inclusiveness of women in leadership.

In a time when even biblical feminist thought did not enjoy the current level of acceptance among evangelicals, the character and determination each exhibited in her accomplishments challenged

184

standing notions of what women could or should want to achieve. Their perseverance, tenacity, and focus influenced others and rallied them to support their causes. Their single-mindedness in working to achieve their vocational calling and their willingness to sacrifice for what they saw as a greater cause assured their success.

These women paid attention to both the practical and the spiritual, providing financial and administrative foundations that would leave their bodies in good stead beyond their lifetimes, so that their denominations were able to stand beyond their death. During their lifetimes, they each acquired substantial real assets-which might rival the current Word of Faith emphasis on material blessing without deliberately articulating a "name it and claim it" theology. Their adherents gave in abundance because they saw the fruit of the labor and wanted to be part of what they saw as "the Lord's work."

In one important sense, however, these four women imbibed and reflected the leadership style of men in that they were generally autocratic and authoritarian in how they seemingly led their respective denominations. While, on the one hand, they promoted equality between men and women, they still acted within a hierarchical model, in which they held the top position and wielded power based primarily on their charismatic personalities. Within this framework, even with so-called governing bodies to support them, these women more or less "dictated" doctrine and institutional polity based on what they believed God revealed to them personally. So they failed to foster replication of the necessary qualities to sustain the legacy of women's leadership within each denomination or allow this leadership pattern to be reproduced in sister Pentecostal denominations.

Though in many ways, these were strong women, responsibilities exacted large tolls on their physical and emotional health. All four died at relatively young ages. In doing all they did, they failed to care for themselves. Three of the women succumbed before reaching the age

185

of sixty. Tate died at fifty-nine, McPherson at fifty-four, and Robinson at fifty-five. Crawford died at age sixty-four.

They all spent inordinate amounts of time on the road, caring for fledgling congregations as well as pastoring their growing local congregations. Although they had ample support, they found it difficult to turn over the personal care of these local bodies to others. Each felt somehow obligated to nurture her scattered congregations. The toll for this attention was these leaders' lives. They, literally, wore themselves out for the sake of their ministries, maintaining travel schedules that kept them on the road several days, weeks, or months out of each year and preaching several times each week. As their ministries grew, they also had responsibility for overseeing and nurturing new works. Even as they appointed other individuals and invested them with jurisdictional oversight, Tate and Robinson still found it necessary or desirable to personally visit several of the fledgling congregations, and McPherson continued to regularly make evangelistic tours. Both Tate and Robinson were carrying out such visits when they died.

McPherson was probably the most negatively, and certainly most visibly, impacted by the strain of ministry responsibilities. She was given to bouts of depression, she is suspected of having had a nervous breakdown, and her death—though ruled an accidental overdose by the coroner—has been questioned by some as a possible suicide.[4] Tate's death from frostbite contracted while on a preaching engagement, and the complications of diabetes, was more than likely preventable. Robinson simply seemed to have worn herself out and died suddenly from exhaustion. Little is known of the circumstances of Crawford's death. Presumably, she died peacefully in her sleep.

Ironically, Crawford, Tate, McPherson, and Robinson prayed for hundreds of people who were healed of a variety of conditions and who attributed their healings to the ministration of these women. Each

186

was, in her way, a proponent of divine healing and this was a core belief of the ministries of both Tate and McPherson. Both Crawford and Tate had even insinuated that reliance on medical resources other than prayer evidenced a lack of faith. Nevertheless, none seemed to exercise her healing gifts on her own behalf or take the necessary steps to take care of her own health. In the end, the same spiritual resources that each had expended on behalf of others, time after time, proved unable to save her own life.

A Final Word

Florence Louise Crawford, Mary Magdalena Lewis Tate, Aimee Semple McPherson, and Ida Bell Robinson, convinced that they had experienced an undeniable call of God to the ministry and leadership of the church, set out to make that call a reality. They individually mounted personal challenges co gender bias in ministry in the early Pentecostal movement—and the Christian church—and won. The variety of their life circumstances indicates their resourcefulness in successfully overcoming gender bias to accomplish their respective ministry goals. Theologically self-taught, and in some cases untaught, they were able to add a feminine voice to the deposit of Pentecostal doctrine and history. Their examples lend support to renewed efforts of Pentecostal and Charismatic women in particular, Evangelical women in general, and more broadly women throughout the church to make a place for themselves either in or alongside the existing church hierarchy—even where gender bias has begun to reappear in the very denominations that some of these women have launched.

These four acted on their Pentecostal beliefs that, as women, they were equally empowered by God through Holy Spirit baptism to fully respond to their vision of ministry. They did not seek permission to preach the gospel. Nor did they seek to change the existing denominations by forcing a place for women's leadership within them.

187

They did not attempt to provide pointed answers to the purported biblical sanctions limiting women's in church leadership. Instead, they based their authority to preach and lead on an understanding that their ministry, like that of their male colleagues, was authenticated by God's stamp of approval on them evidenced in the outpouring and infilling of God's Spirit. They understood themselves as having the same empowerment that infilling brought and the same impartation of spiritual gifts to carry the same message. They knew that they too had been sanctified and made fit vessels for God's use. They too had spoken in tongues as evidence of their infilling. They too had laid hands on the sick and afflicted for healing and deliverance. They too had paid the high price of being mistreated as the people of God. They had sown and they had reaped a harvest-and no one could deny the fruit of their ministry. In acknowledging their calls, they intentionally created environments where they and (in two cases) other women could be free to wholeheartedly pursue their God-given call to ministry and leadership, as individuals endowed with an abundance of spiritual gifts-preaching, teaching, administration, and evangelism. They were able to demonstrate emphatically that women were equally called and empowered to minister and to lead the church.

These four women spoke out on issues about which they felt strongly. Crawford was vocal about what she saw as the loss of emphasis on sanctification. Tate was insistent that most other churches claimed what she felt were unbiblical titles for themselves. McPherson was adamant about the need for moderation within Pentecostal worship. Robinson was outspokenly set against American involvement in World War II. They were noticeably less vocal concerning the limitations placed on the leadership of women in the Pentecostal movement.

They were less vocal, but not less articulate, on the issue of women's leadership, for theirs was a lived feminism. They simply went

188

about doing what they felt free to do, understanding intuitively that a full-frontal attack on rigidly held ideas about women's place would have done little good. They also understood that such an effort might cost them energy they could more fruitfully expend in doing what they felt called to do. Without asking permission or making excuses, they accomplished what few others—either women or men-were able. They built congregations from the ground up, bodies they successfully led and developed into viable denominations that stand today as a testimony to the success of their practical feminism.

Notes

Preface

1. Mark Chavez, Ordaining Women: Culture and Conflict in Religious Organizations (Cambridge, MA: Harvard University Press, 1997), 16-17.

2. Such as bishop, presiding elder, overseer, or other jurisdictional or administrative leader.

3. Chavez, Ordaining Women, 2-3.

4. See Charles Barfoot and Gerald Sheppard. "Prophetic vs. Priestly Religion: The Changing Role of Women Ministers in Classical Pentecostal Churches," *Review of Religious Research* 21 (summer 1980): 2-17; Letha Scanzoni and Susan Setta, "Women in Evangelical, Holiness, and Pentecostal Traditions 1900-1968, " in vol. 3 of *Women in Religion in America*, ed. Rosemary Radford Ruether and Rosemary Skinner Keller (Cambridge, Mass.: Harper and Row Publishers, 1986); and David Roebuck, "Limiting Liberty: The Church of God and Women Ministers," 1886-1996 (doctoral dissertation, Vanderbilt University, Nashville, TN, 1999).

5. The organization which has intermittently use the terms "Apostolic Faith" and "Apostolic Faith Mission" to identify itself, now uses "Apostolic Faith Church." There is no indication of when the change in name was made.

6. Social scientists use this typology in a variety of contexts. Among them are Hans Baer and Merrill Singer, African-American Religion in the Twentieth Century: Varieties of Protest and Accommodation (Knoxville: University of Tennessee Press, 1992); Adam Fairclough, Better Day Coming: Blacks and Equality, 1890-2000 (New York: Viking Press, 2001); Ellen Carol DuBois "The Radicalism of the Woman Suffrage Movement: Notes toward the Reconstruction of Nineteenth-Century Feminism," and Joan Tronto "Changing Goals and Changing Strategies: Varieties of Women's Political Activities," both in U.S. Women in Struggle: A Feminist Studies Anthology, ed Claire Goldberg Moses and Heidi I. Hartmann (Urbana, IL: University of Illinois Press, 1995).

Introduction

I. Virginia Bereton and Christa Rissmeyer Klein, "American Women in Ministry: A History of Protestant Beginning Points," in *Women in American Religion*, ed. Janet Wilson James, 175 (Philadelphia: University of Pennsylvania Press, 1980).

2. This view holds that women can be leaders in ministry as long as a man is in the head leadership position. Women therefore are the complement or the helper of the man.

3. Max Weber, *Sociology of Religion*, trans. E. Fischoff (Boston: Peabody Press, 1963), 103-5.

4. See Charles Barfoot and Gerald Sheppard, "Prophetic vs. Priestly Religion: The Changing Role of Women Ministers in Classical Pentecostal Churches," *Review of Religious* Research 21 (Summer 1980): 2- 17.

5. Three works give an accounting of Parham's life and ministry: James R. Goff, *Fields White unto Harvest: Charles F. Parham and the Missionary Origins of Pentecostalism* (Fayetteville: University of Arkansas Press, 1988); Sarah E. Parham, *The Life of Charles F. Parham: Founder of the Apostolic Faith Movement* (New York: Garland Publishing, 1985); and Vinson Synan, *The Holiness-Pentecostal Tradition: Charismatic Movements of the Twentieth Century* (Grand Rapids: Wm B. Eerdmans, 1997).

6. Goff, *Fields White unto Harvest*, 54- 55.

7. Robert Mapes Anderson, *Vision of the Disinherited: The Making of American Pentecostalism* (Peabody, MA.: Hendrickson Publishers, 1979), 61.

8. *Los Angeles Times*, April 18, 1906, 1.

9. Frank Bartleman, *Azusa Street* (Plainfield, NJ: Logos International, 1980), 54.

10. Walter Hollenweger, *The Pentecostals: The Charismatic Movement in the Churches*. (Minneapolis: Augsburg Press, 1972), 24.

11. David Roebuck, "Loose the Women," *Christian History* 58, 17:2 (1998), 38.

12. Parham, *Life of Charles F. Parham*, 53.

13. See Agnes N. O. LaBerge, *What God Hath Wrought* (New York: Garland Press, 1985. Originally published by Herald Publishing, Chicago, 1920).

14. "Clara Lum," in the *Dictionary of Pentecostal and Charismatic Movements*, ed. Stanley M. Burgess, Gary R. McGee, and Patrick H. Alexander (Grand Rapids, MI: Zondervan Publishing, 1988), 561.

15. Ted Olsen, "American Pentecost: The Story Behind the Azusa Street Revival, the Most Phenomenal Event of Twentieth Century Christianity," *Christian History* 58117 no. 2 (1998), 14.

16. For a detailed discussion of the contribution of women to the Azusa Street Revival, see Estrelda Alexander, *The Women of Azusa Street* (Cleveland: Pilgrim Press, 2005).

17. See Elaine Lawless, God's *Peculiar People: Women's Voices and Folk Tradition in a Pentecostal Church* (Lexington: University of Kentucky Press, 1988), 6.

18. Roebuck, "Loose the Women," 39.

19. See, Chavez, *Ordaining Women*, 2- 3.

20. Ibid., 16.

21. Ibid. , 17.

22. Edith Blumhofer, "Women in Evangelicalism and Pentecostalism", in *Women and Church: The Challenge of Ecumenical Solidarity in an Age of Alienation*, ed. Melanie May (New York: William B. Eerdmans, 1991), 4.

23. In "Priestly vs. Prophetic Religion," Barfoot and Sheppard contend that "to many mainline denominations, Pentecostalism was scandalous because of its shift away from traditional patriarchalism", 3.

24. *The Weekly Evangel*, 131 (March 18, 1916), 6.

25. David Roebuck alludes to this pattern of deployment in the Church of God (Cleveland, Tenn.) in "Limiting Liberty: The Church of God and Women Ministers, 1886-1996," doctoral dissertation, Vanderbilt University, Nashville, TN: 1999, 125.

26. Both the Assemblies of God and Church of God took this stance for several years.

27. See Ithiel Clemmons, *Bishop C. H. Mason and the Roots of the Church of God in Christ* (Bakersfield, CA: Pneuma Life Publishers, 1996).

28. Ibid., 109.

29. Ibid., 101-2.

30. Ibid., 109. Emphasis mine.

31. These terms do not carry the meaning of one who travels to different locations to win others to Christ. These women worked inside local churches.

32. *Minutes of the General Council of the Assembly of God*, 1914, 13- 16.

33. *Executive Presbytery Minutes of the General Council of the Assembly of God*, November 23, 1914, I.

34. *Minutes of the General Council*, 1917, 6.

35. *Minutes of the General Council*, 1919, 7.

36. *Minutes of the General Council*, 1920, 48.

37. These women were considered clergy-pastors, missionaries, and evangelists-too and were ordained to the "full gospel ministry." What was withheld was the right to perform sacraments, to vote or participate in governance, and to participate in institutional leadership.

38. "General Council Special Rule", 1922, 1.

39. *Minutes of the General Council*, 1935, 111.

40. Church of God of Prophecy, "General Assembly Minutes, 1907," in *General Assembly Minutes*, 1906-1914: Photographic Reproduction of the First Ten General Assembly Minutes (Cleveland, TN: White Wing Publishing, 1992), 13.

41. Ibid., 21.

42. "Third General Assembly Minutes, 1908," in *General Assembly Minutes*, 49.

43. "Fourth General Assembly Minutes, 1909," in *General Assembly Minutes*, 63. This argument was maintained until 2000, when it granted women limited ordination-without full clergy rights. It denied them access to the bishopric-its highest rank of ministry as well as the opportunity to serve in most institutional leadership positions.

44. Seventh General Assembly Minutes, 1912, in *General Assembly Minutes*, 133.

45. Eighth General Assembly Minutes, 1913, in *General Assembly Minutes*, 228.

46. Twelfth General Assembly Minutes, 1916, in *General Assembly Minutes* 242.

47. Twentieth General Assembly Minutes, 1926, in *General Assembly Minutes* 109. No explanation was provided of what that work would be.

48. Maria Woodward-Etter, *A Diary of Signs and Wonders* (Tulsa, OK: Harrison House, 1980; originally published 1916 by author).

49. "Did You Know: Little Known and Remarkable Facts about Pentecostalism," *Christian History* 58, 1/17, no. 2 (1998), 3.

50. Ibid., 627.

51. See the autobiographical work of Carrie Judd Montgomery, *Under His Wing: The Life and Teaching of Carrie Judd Montgomery* (New York: Garland Publishing, 1985).

52. See Beth Prim Howell, *Lady on a Donkey* (New York: Dutton, 1960); Lester Sumrall, *Lillian Trasher: the Nile Mother* (Springfield, MO: Gospel Publishing House, 1951); and Charles W. Conn, Where the Saints Have Trod (Cleveland, TN: Pathway Press, 1959), 15- 16.

53. Barfoot and Sheppard, "Priestly vs. Prophetic Religion," 9-10.

54. Ibid., 10.

55. Letha Scanzoni and Susan Setta. "Women in Evangelical, Holiness, and Pentecostal Traditions" in *Women in Religion in America*, vol. 3, 1900-1968, ed. Rosemary Ruether and Rosemary Keller (Cambridge, MA: Harper and Row, 1981), 229.

56. Ibid.

57. Ibid.

58. Edith Blumhofer, *The Assemblies of God: A Chapter in the Story of American Pentecostalism*, Volume I-to 1941 (Springfield, MO: Gospel Publishing, 1989), 357.

59. Barfoot and Sheppard, "Priestly vs. Prophetic Religion", 16.

60. Ibid.

Florence Crawford

1. "Florence Crawford," in Stanley M. Burgess, Gary Magee, and Patrick H. Alexander, *Dictionary of Pentecostal and Charismatic Movements* (Grand Rapids, MI.: Zondervan Publishing, 1988), 229. See also Apostolic Faith Mission, A Historical Account of the Apostolic Faith, a Trinitarian-Fundamental Evangelistic Organization: Its Origin, Functions, Doctrinal Heritage, and Departmental Activities of Evangelism (Portland, OR.: Apostolic Faith Publishing House, 1965).

2. Apostolic Faith Mission, *Historical Account*, 54.

3. Ibid., 55.

4. Ibid., 55- 56.

5. Raymond Crawford, *The Light of Life Brought Triumph: A Brief Sketch of the Life and Labors of Florence L. (Mother) Crawford*, commemorative edition (Portland OR: Apostolic Faith Publishing House, 1955), 3-4.

6. Apostolic Faith Mission, *Historical Account*, 57.

7. Florence Crawford, "Christian Living," October 11, 1931.

8. Florence Crawford, *Greater Than Solomon: Sermons and Scriptural Studies, Book One* (Portland, OR: Apostolic Faith Mission, n.d., 53-54.

9. Apostolic Faith Mission, *Historical Account*, 59.

10. "A Witness to the Power of God," *Higher Way* (June - Sept, 2006), 8.

11. Crawford, *The Light of Light Brought Triumph*, 9.

12. Apostolic Faith 1/3 (Nov. 1906), 3.

13. Ibid., 2.

14. Untitled article, Apostolic Faith, 1/2 (Oct 1906), 3.

15. Early evangelical historiography often omitted the wife's first name, even when the couple was equally involved in ministry.

16. Untitled article, Apostolic Faith 1/2 (Oct. 1906), 1.

17. "San Francisco and Oakland," *Apostolic Faith*, 1/4 (Dec. 1906), 4.

195

18. "From Azusa to Portland: A Look Back," *Higher Way* 99/1 (Jan.- Mar., 2006), 14.

19. Ithiel Clemmons, *Bishop C.H. Mason and the Roots of the Church of God in Christ* (Bakersfield, CA.: Pneuma Life Publishers, 1996), 50.

20. Larry Martin, ed. *Doctrines and Disciplines of the Azusa Street Mission of Los Angeles California,* The Complete Azusa Street Library, vol. 7 Joplin, MO: Christian Life Books, 2000), 110.

21. Crawford, *Light of Life*, 19.

22. "The Founding of Our Work" http//www.apostolicfaith.org/afc church/founding.htm.

23. "From Azusa to Portland: A Look Back," *Higher Way* 99/1 Jan.- Mar., 2006), 14.

24. Amos Morgan, *Choosing Separate Ways*, unpublished manuscript, 2006.

25. Apostolic Faith Mission, *Historical Account*, 198.

26. Ibid., 232.

27. Untitled article, Apostolic Faith 33 (July, 1916?), 2, cited in Deno, "God Authority and the Home," 96.

28. Deno, "God Authority and the Home, 96.

29. "Camp Meeting," Time (August 19, 1935), 34- 35.

30. Personal interview with Amos Morgan, December 12, 2006.

31. "Camp Meeting," Time, 34-35.

32. See Cecil M. Robeck, "Florence Crawford," in *Portraits of a Generation: Early Pentecostal Leaders*, ed. James R. Goff Jr. and Grant Wacker (Fayetteville: University of Arkansas Press, 2002), 45.

33. Correspondence from Amos Morgan, May 1, 2007.

34. Apostolic Faith Mission, Historical Account, 71.

35. For a discussion of the residual effect of Crawford's leadership on the ministry of women in the Open Standard Church, see Robert Mitchell, *Heritage and Horizons: The History of the Open Bible Standard Churches* (Des Moines, IA: Open Bible Standard Churches, 1982), 47-48.

36. The name of the publication was changed to The Light of Hope in 1981 and to Higher Way in 1995. Sometime during that period, it was also changed to a magazine format.

37. Deno, "God Authority and the Home," 83.

38. Florence Crawford, "Does God Call Women to Preach the Gospel As Well As Men?" *The Apostolic Faith* 18 (Winter 1911), 2.

39. The Apostolic Faith, "Women Preachers," tract, Portland, Oregon, 3.

40. Ibid., 4.

41. "San Francisco and Oregon" *Apostolic Faith* 1/4,(December, 1906), 4.

42. Deno, "God Authority and the Home," 91.

43. Correspondence from Amos Morgan, April, 21, 2007.

44. According to an interview with Morgan, both Mildred and Virginia were sidelined because neither was willing or able to live up to the rigid moral standard imposed by Crawford on those who worked alongside her.

45. Deno, "God Authority and the Home," 92.

46. Ibid., 97.

47. Ibid.

Mary Magdalena Lewis Tate

1. Wardell Payne, ed., *Directory of African American Religious Bodies: a Compendium by the Howard University School of Divinity*, 2nd ed. (Washington, D.: Howard University Press, 1995), 95.

2. Some sources place her birth date as January 3 and others January 5. While most sources cite her place of birth as Dickson, Tennessee, others place it at Clarksville, thirty-three miles to the north.

3. Sources record that two of her sisters were to play important roles in her ministry. No mention is made of the third sister.

4. Most of the scant biographical materials confirm this fact, but none of it says specifically what type of education she received.

5. Telephone interview with Meharry Lewis, October 6, 2001.

6. Helen M. and Meharry H. Lewis, *Seventy-fifth Anniversary Yearbook of the Church of the Living God, Pillar and Ground of the Truth 1903-1978* (Nashville: New and Living Way Publishing, 1978), 5.

7. Geraldine Manning, "World Within, World Without: A New Vision," DMin. thesis, Wesley Theological Seminary, Washington, DC, 1996, 109.

8. Helen M. and Meharry L. Lewis, *The Beauty of Holiness: A Small Catechism of the Holiness Faith and Doctrine* (Nashville: New and Living Way Publishing, 1988), 83-86.

197

9. Manning, "World Within, World Without," 109.

10. Lewis and Lewis, *Seventy-fifth Anniversary Yearbook*, 5.

11. Tate divided the denomination administratively into state jurisdictions and appointed bishops under her supervision to oversee planting and operation of the individual congregations.

12. Lewis and Lewis, *Seventy-fifth Anniversary Yearbook*, 5.

13. Telephone interview with Meharry H. Lewis, October 6, 2001.

14. The "Petition for the Charter of the Church of the Living God, Pillar and Ground of the Truth," filed with the Chatham County (Georgia) Superior Court on February 9, 1911, shows Estes as a signatory. Mary Magdalena Tate Collection, Moorland-Spingarn Research Center, Howard University Library, Howard University, Washington, DC.

15. Felix E. Lewis, "Who Is Truth?" *The True Report* 112 (August 10, 1929), 4.

16. Manning, "World Within, World Without," 109.

17. Ibid.

18. "Church of the Living God; Christian Workers for Fellowship" in *New Catholic Dictionary*, ed. Conde Pallen and John J. Wynne (New York: Universal Knowledge Foundation, 1929), xx.

19. The term "holiness bands" refers to loosely organized groups, generally members of other organized congregations, who met for prayer, Bible study, worship, and teaching usually in homes of individuals. Members generally remained, at least temporarily, in their own churches for regular Sunday worship services. Participation in a band was generally a precursor to starting a new congregation.

20. Mary Frances Lewis Keith, who had remarried by that time, took over the Keith Dominion; Helen Middleton Lewis succeeded her husband, Felix E. Lewis, as head of the Lewis Dominion upon his death.

21. A review of annual programs from annual General Assemblies of the denomination and its successors reveals biographies, testimonials, and agendas with several persons named Lewis who have filled leadership roles at various levels of the church.

22. When the Pentecostal movement started in full in 1906, many holiness adherents adopted the doctrine of speaking in tongues as initial evidence of Holy Spirit baptism.

23. Lewis and Lewis, *Seventy-fifth Anniversary Yearbook*, 8.

24. Ibid.

25. See The Constitution, *Government and General Decree Book of the Church of the Living God, the Pillar and Ground of the Truth* (Incorporated) (Chattanooga, TN: New and Living Way Publishing, 1924).

26. Ibid., 6.

27. *Seventy-fifth Anniversary Yearbook*, 8.

28. See Willie Ray, *A Man in Touch with God* (Detroit: Ray and Hunter, 1981). Sources do not indicate the nature of the schism.

29. Constitution, Government and General Decree Book, 49.

30. Little information is available about the church's foreign activity.

31. Felton Best, "Breaking the Gender Barrier," in Felton Best *Black Religious Leadership from the Slave Community to the Million Man March: Flames of Fire*, Black Studies vol. 3 (Lewiston, NY: Edwin Mellen Press, 1998), 163.

32. It is unclear which of the 254 hymns Tate wrote. The cover page bears the inscription "compiled by Bishop M. L. Tate and edited by Bishop M. F. L. Keith." In the preface, Keith writes, "This Hymn Book represents the work and labor of our dear Mother M. L. Tate."

33. Jon Michael Spencer, *Black Hymnody: A Hymnological History of the African-American Church* (Knoxville: University of Tennessee Press, 1992), 134.

34. Ibid.

35. Hugh J. Roberts, "Spiritual Songs and Hymns: A Review" *Journal of Black Sacred Music* 2 (fall 1988), 88-95.

36. This includes the *Decree Book* published in 1914 and the Constitution published in 1923.

37. As detailed in Lewis and Lewis, *Beauty of Holiness*, 10. Tate's followers cite the Methodist Church as specifically corrupting the proper name for God's true church.

38. *Constitution, Government and General Decree Book*, 23, 29, and 50. 39. Ibid., 29-31, 65-66.

40. Ibid., 66.

41. Ibid., 9.

42. Ibid., 25.

43. Lewis and Lewis, Seventy-fifth Anniversary Yearbook, 23.

44. At that time, however, the denomination was still primarily relegated to the East Coast. This partitioning, in fact, gave each chief overseer specific jurisdiction over further growth within his or her respective dominion.

45. See The House of God Which Is the Church of the Living God, the Pillar and Ground of the Truth, without Controversy, Inc., *The Constitution, Government, and General Decree Book*, 3rd rev. ed. (Philadelphia, 1936), 93-107. Even here, there is controversy; the Keith Dominion later contends its name, the House of God Which Is the Church of the Living God, the Pillar and Ground of the Truth without Controversy, is the initial name Tate chose for her organization but that other factions obliterated records that verify that fact.

46. Lewis and Lewis, *The Beauty of Holiness*, 9.

47. Ibid., 10.

48. Ibid., 83.

49. For example, all of these titles are used in various sections of the *Constitution, Government and General Decree Book*.

50. See Lewis and Lewis, *Beauty of Holiness*, 17-23.

51. *Constitution, Government and General Decree Book*, 49. Upholding Old Testament legal and feast custom was an element that was unique with Tate's organization.

52. Roberts, "Spiritual Songs," 93.

53. This goes to the point of abstaining from medicines that contain alcohol or habit-forming drugs.

54. *Constitution, Government and General Decree Book*, 37. This requirement goes beyond most Pentecostal denominations that encourage their members to seek Holy Spirit Baptism but do not withhold membership from those who do not receive it.

55. Lewis and Lewis, *The Beauty of Holiness*, ix (emphasis my own).

56. Sherry Dupree, for example, makes that contention in her introduction to chapter 9, "Women Founder and Leaders," in *African-American Holiness Pentecostal Movement: An Annotated Bibliography* (New York: Garland Press, 1996), 509.

57. Tate's grandson, Meharry Lewis, current presiding bishop of the Lewis Dominion, makes such a contention.

58. Dupree, *African American Holiness Pentecostal Movement*, 509. Most Pentecostals, however, consider Christian Science doctrine heretical. Tate's biographer, Meharry Lewis, suggests that apparent influences from Eddy are merely coincidental.

59. Interview with Meharry Lewis, August 22, 2002.

60. Lewis and Lewis, *Seventy-Fifth Anniversary Yearbook*, 16.

61. Ibid., 15.

62. A problem in tracing the pattern of deployment is that church records often identify people only by initials. Further identification can sometimes be determined by the pronouns employed in descriptions. In some instances, pictures are available.

63. *The Constitution and Decree Book* indicates that Scott subsequently broke relationship with the organization and attempted to charter a new congregation, 60.

64. *Official Manual of the Church of the Living God Pillar and Ground of the Truth, without Controversy*, 1993. Quoted in Best, "Breaking the Gender Barrier," 167.

65. She had been married to Tate's older son, Walter, who died prematurely. Though she remarried, she maintained a close relationship with her former mother-in-law.

66. Lewis and Lewis, *Seventy-Fifth Anniversary Yearbook*, 10-11.

67. "The Church at Atlantic Beach, Florida," Lewis and Lewis, *Seventy-fifth Anniversary Yearbook*, 38.

68. Ibid., 16.

69. Meharry Lewis, *Mary Lena Lewis Tate: A Street Called Straight*, un-published manuscript, 31.

70. Details of the charges from both sides are reported in *The True Report* 112 (September, 1929), 1-4 .

71. Best, "Breaking the Gender Barrier," 163.

72. Church of the Living God, Inc. *Our General Assembly*, October, 1977, 1-2, 29.

73. She later remarried, taking Jewell as a surname.

74. Dupree, *African-American Holiness Pentecostal Movement*, 149-50 and "Black Trinitarian Pentecostals" Encylopeida.com https://www.encyclopedia.com/ religion/ encyclopedias-almanacs-transcripts-and-maps/black-trinitarian-pentecostals

75. Lewis and Lewis, *The Beauty of Holiness*, 61.

76. Ibid.

77. Ibid. , 62.

78. Ken Pellis, "Pioneer of Holiness Church Finds Rewards in Work" *The Palm Beach Post*, Saturday, April 9, 1988, 2.

79. Ibid.

80. Dupree, *African-American Holiness Pentecostal Movement*, 149.

81. Payne, *Directory of African American Religious Bodies*, 175.

82. Charles E. Jones, *Black Holiness. A Guide to the Study of Black Participation in Wesleyan Perfectionist and Glossolalic Pentecostal Movements* (Metuchen, NJ: Scarecrow Press, 1987), 117.

83. Payne, *Directory of African American Religious Bodies*, 176.

84. A substantial recent work on Tate is Kelly Mendiola's 2002 dissertation at the University of Texas, Austin, "The Hand of Woman: Four Holiness-Pentecostal Evangelists and American Culture, 1840-1930."

85. For example, Tate's emphasis on Sabbath keeping mistakenly identifies Sunday instead of Saturday as the true Sabbath, without providing theological rationale for such a switch. See "If We Work Six Days, the Seventh Day Is Sabbath," Mary Magdalena Tate Collection, Moorland-Spingarn Research Center, n.d., n.p.

86. For example, J. Vernon McGee, a fundamentalist national radio Bible teacher, popular in many evangelical circles during the 1980s and 1990s, could often be heard dismissing the validity of women as pastoral leaders on the grounds that women were easily led into heresy, citing the likes of Eddy, White, and Cox. It is possible that he was completely unaware of Tate and her work.

87. Meharry Lewis, "Mary Lena Tate: VISION!" in *Church of the Living God, the Pillar and Ground of the Truth, Founders Day Recognition: Our 89th Year*, January 25, 1992, 4.

Aimee Semple McPherson

1. Vinson Synan, *The Twentieth Century Pentecostal Explosion*. (Altamonte Springs, FL.: Creation House, 1987), 100.

2. Edith Blumhofer, "Sister," *Christian History* 58, 17/2 (spring, 1998), 32.

3. McPherson's style belied the staid attire of most Pentecostal women, changing over the years to a more stylish appearance capped, towards the end of her life, with a facelift.

4. Edith Blumhofer, *Aimee Semple McPherson: Everybody's Sister* (Grand Rapids: William B. Eerdmans, 1993), 16.

5. She characterized the disappearance as an abduction, but it was challenged in the courts as a lover's tryst.

6. According to Gregg D. Townsend in "The Material Dream of Aimee Semple McPherson," *Pneuma* 14 (spring 1992), 171-83, the early Salvation Army ties were

reflected in McPherson's emphasis on social outreach. According to Nathaniel Van Cleave in *The Vine and the Branches: The History of the International Church of the Foursquare Gospel* (Los Angeles: International Church of the Foursquare Gospel), 1992, the Salvationist influence gave McPherson an affinity for the military type uniforms many of her workers wore and for use of military terminology.

7. In a 1934 debate with Baptist fundamentalist Ben Bogard on divine healing, McPherson referred to historical figures such as Justin Martyr, Luther, and Wesley. See *McPherson-Bogard Debate* (Decatur, GA: Thrasher Publications, 2000), 18.

8. Aimee Semple McPherson, *The Story of My Life* (Waco, TX: Word Publications, 1973), 25. Originally published in 1951 by Echo Park Evangelistic Association, Los Angeles.

9. Hannah, barren wife of Penuel, prayed for a child and promised to devote that child to God's service. God answered her prayer by giving her a son, Samuel, whom she left at the temple in God's service with the prophet Eli. Samuel became one of the great prophets of Israel.

10. Aimee Semple McPherson, *This Is That* (Los Angeles: Echo Park Evangelistic Association, 1923), 14.

11. McPherson, *Story of My Life*, 30.

12. Ibid., 32-35.

13. Her "ministry" involved primarily singing, playing the piano, or praying with seekers and new converts, helping set up and take down tents and chairs before and after a meeting, helping to prepare meals, and washing dishes.

14. McPherson, *The Story of My Life*, 71.

15. Ibid., 74-75.

16. In a movement vehemently opposed to divorce (especially in the early period), McPherson was twice divorced.

17. Howard Kenyon, "An Analysis of Ethical Issues in the History of the Assemblies of God," PhD dissertation, Baylor University, 1988, 214.

18. Brumbeck, Carl. *Suddenly from Heaven; a History of the Assemblies of God* (Springfield, Mo.: Gospel Publishing House, 1961), 272.

19. McPherson was at odds with other Pentecostals for not drawing strict denominational lines.

20. Townsend, "Material Dream," 180.

21. This was initially to be a voluntary association that complemented rather than replaced members' participation in existing denominations. Gradually,

however, it became a closely organized association that eventually grew into a denomination.

22. Daniel M. Epstein, *Sister Aimee: The Life of Amy Semple McPherson* (New York: Harcourt, Brace, Jovanovich, 1993), 233.

23. McPherson presents Christ as Savior, Baptizer in the Holy Spirit, Healer, and Coming King. She claimed this formula was revealed to her while meditating on the Book of Ezekiel in preparation for a message she preached in Oakland, California.

24. Donald Dayton, *The Theological Roots of Pentecostalism* (Grand Rapids: Francis Asbury, 1987), 20-23.

25. Albert B. Simpson, *The Four-Fold Gospel* (New York: Christian Alliance Publishing, 1925). Simpson used the terminology for what he saw as the four basic tenets of the gospel: Christ the Savior, Healer, Sanctifier, and Soon Coming King. Though an avid reader of Simpson, McPherson alleged that she had no knowledge of his formulation, according to Van Cleave's account in The Vine and the Branches, 7.

26. McPherson, Aimee Semple, *The Personal Testimony of Aimee Semple McPherson* (Paramount, Calif.: Foursquare Mission Press, 1997), 55.

27. Ezekiel 1:4-24.

28. These symbols serve as the foundation for the corporate logo of the International Church of the Foursquare Gospel.

29. McPherson, *Personal Testimony*, 55-56.

30. Blumhofer, *Everybody's Sister*, 279.

31. McPherson held that healing, like salvation, was provided in the atonement. Others took a more cautious approach, seeing that although healing was available to all believers, not everyone would be healed. While McPherson believed that divine healing could happen over a period of time, others taught that it was instantaneous by definition.

32. For a discussion of her moderate stance, see Matthew A. Sutton, "Between the Refrigerator and the Wildfire: Aimee Semple McPherson, Pentecostalism, and the Fundamentalist-Modernist Controversy," *Church History* 72:1 (Mar. 2003), 159-88.

33. Durasoff, Steve, *Bright Wind of the Spirit: Pentecostalism Today* (Englewood Cliffs, NJ: Prentice-Hall, 1972), 71.

34. *Story of My Life*, 137.

35. The name is derived from the concept of the church as the Bride of Christ waiting to be raptured, or called out of the earthly realm at the last day.

36. Her first autobiographical work, *This Is That,* appeared in 1923. A second, longer, work, *The Story of My Life* was published posthumously in 1979.

37. See L. DeAne Largerquist, "Aimee Semple McPherson," in *Twentieth Century Shapers of American Popular Religion,* ed. Charles H. Lippy (New York: Greenwood Press, 1989), 267; Van Cleave, The Vine and the Branches, 127; Robert Cornwall, "Primitivism and the Redemption of Dispensationalism in the Theology of Aimee Semple McPherson," in *Pneuma* 14 (spring 1992), 25; and Alvyn Austin, *Aimee Semple McPherson* (Don Mills, Ont.: Fitzhenry and Whiteside, 1980), 55. The station was sold by the Foursquare Church for $250,000,000 in 2005.

38. The commissary opened in August 1927. According to William G. McLaughlin in "Aimee Semple McPherson: Your Sister in the King's Glad Service," in *Modern American Protestantism and Its World,* Volume 3: *Women and Women's Issues,* ed. Marty E. Martin (Munich: K.G. Saur, 1993), 134, within eighteen months, it provided forty thousand meals and more than sixteen thousand pieces of clothing.

39. Daniel Epstein, "The Legacy of Aimee Semple McPherson," in *Foursquare World Advance,* 36:6 July/August 2000), 6-9.

40. Durasoff talks of one such meeting in Key West, Florida, in *Bright Wind of the Spirit,* 71. William McLaughlin in "Aimee Semple McPherson: Your Sister in the King's Glad Service," 128, also discusses such meetings that were held in Miami, Florida.

41. Blumhofer, *Everybody's Sister,* 268.

42. L.I.F.E. was the fourth of fifty-one Pentecostal Bible colleges established since 1908, following behind the Church of God Bible Training School (1918), the Pentecostal Holiness Church (1919),and the Assemblies of God (1922). Though many of these schools enjoyed only a short life span, L.I.F.E. continued to grow and became one of the first Bible institutes to offer a full course of studies leading to a bachelor's degree (Th.B.). In 1936, McPherson moved ahead of her peers by offering a Th.D degree.

43. See Van Cleave, *The Vine and the Branches,* 79, and Robert Bahr, *Least of All Saints: The Story of Aimee Semple McPherson* (Englewood Cliffs: Prentice-Hall, 1979), 79.

44. *Lately Thomas, Storming Heaven: the Lives and Turmoils of Minnie Kennedy and Aimee Semple McPherson* (New York: Morrow, 1970), 136-44.

45. Blumhofer, *Everybody's Sister,* 264,319, 333. 46. Ibid., 264.

47. Thomas, *Storming Heaven,* 222- 25.

48. Blumhofer, *Everybody's Sister*, 62-64.

49. Epstein, *Sister Aimee: The Life*, 376-80. 50. Ibid., 419-20.

51. Blumhofer, *Everybody's Sister*, 356. 52. Ibid., 320-21.

53. Dorothy, Parker, "Our Lady of the Loudspeaker," *The New Yorker*, 25 February 1928.

54. Blumhofer, *Everybody's Sister*, 179-83, 235-45.

55. See John J. Kershner, *The Disappearance of Aimee Semple McPherson* (Los Angeles: Gem Publishing, 1926), and Robert V. P. Steele, *The Vanishing Evangelist* (New York, Viking Press, 1959).

56. Including the Los Angeles district attorney, who pursued the case vigorously.

57. Two separate grand jury investigations received extensive coverage across the country. When the first found insufficient evidence of an abduction, McPherson saw the findings as vindication. When further evidence indicated a possible tryst, she maintained her story, accusing the media of conspiracy. Harshest criticism of the episode comes from Nancy Barr Mavity's, *Sister Aimee* (Garden City:, NY: Doubleday, Doran & Co., 1931).

58. Epstein, *Sister Aimee: The Life*, 342-43.

59. The period of the marriage to Hutton is covered in detail in Thomas, Storming Heaven, 225-46, 225-74, and in *Epstein, Sister Aimee: The Life of Aimee Semple McPherson*, 364-83.

60. Blumhofer, *Everybody's Sister*, 333.

61. Ibid., 142-44.

62. Wayne E. Warner, "Open Standard Bible Churches," in *New International Dictionary of Pentecostal and Charismatic Movements*, 945-46.

63. Ibid., 945.

64. Largerquist, "Aimee *Semple McPherson,*" 268.

65. Van Cleave, *Vine and the Branches*, 45.

66. Aimee Semple McPherson, "Class Notes on the Book of Acts," Los Angeles: L.I.F.E. Bible College, n.d., 30. Cited in Charles Barfoot and Gerald Sheppard. "Prophetic vs. Priestly Religion: The Changing Role of Women Ministers in Classical Pentecostal Churches," *Review of Religious Research* 21 (Summer 1980): 15.

67. McPherson, "Class Notes," 27. Cited in Barfoot and Shephard, "Prophetic vs. Priestly Religion," 9.

68. Aimee Semple McPherson, untitled article in Bridal Call 2f2 July, 1927), 7. Cited in Barfoot and Shephard, "Prophetic vs. Priestly Religion," 15.

69. Lately, *Storming Heaven*, 13.

70. Van Cleave, *Vine and the Branches*, 42.

71. McPherson contended that Rheba Crawford, McPherson's assistant pastor for a year, preferred the arrangement, insisting that "there was not enough room for two stars on the platform," and that this preference kept Crawford off the podium with her. See McPherson, *Story of My Life*, 245.

72. Blumhofer, *Everybody's Sister*, 205.

73. McPherson, *Story of My Life*, 18.

74. Van Cleave, *Vine and the Branches*, 39, 51, and Blumhofer, *Everybody's Sister*, 256-57, 349-55, and 362-70.

75. Van Cleave, *Vine and the Branches*, 51.

76. Blumhofer, *Everybody's Sister*, 252-78, and Epstein, *Sister Aimee: The Life*, 390-416.

77. Epstein, *Sister Aimee: The Life*, 391.

78. Alvyn Austin, *Aimee Semple McPherson*, (Don Mills, Ont: Fitzhenry and Whiteside, 1980), 58, and *Everybody's Sister*, 416.

79. McPherson, *Story of My Life*, 247.

80. Epstein, *Sister Aimee* 381-82.

81. Thomas, *Storming Heaven*, 333.

82. Epstein, *Sister Aimee* 419.

83. Blumhofer, Everybody's Sister, 360-36.

84. Van Cleave, *Vine and the Branches*, 40-41

85. For a discussion of these women, see ibid.

86. McPherson dubbed these women "city sisters." For a discussion of their contribution to McPherson's ministry, see Townsend, "Material Dream," 176-83.

87. Townsend, "Material Dream," 177.

88. Blumhofer, Everybody's Sister, 361. While no reason has been publicly given, the decline in women's leadership in the Foursquare Church follows the general pattern Pentecostal pattern. Since McPherson put no strategies in place to maintain women's leadership, it is not surprising.

89. "Denominational Statement Regarding Women in Public Ministry," adopted February 18, 1975, International Church of the Foursquare Gospel Convention, Los Angeles, California.

90. *Foursquare World Advance* (May/June 1998), 2.

91. "Women in Ordained Leadership Ministry," a position statement for the International Church of the Foursquare Gospel, available online at www.foursquare.org/files/denominational_statement.

92. Many women do serve, however, as copastors on husband-wife teams.

93. Van Cleave, *Vine and the Branches*, 41-43.

94. While McPherson's group is considered an orthodox Pentecostal denomination, Christian Science is considered heretical by most other Christian traditions.

95. Eileen W. Lindner, ed. *The Yearbook of American and Canadian Churches*, Vol. 75, 2007 (Nashville, Abingdon Press), 378.

96. This characterization was not found in the original book by Nathaniel West, published by Random House in 1939.

97. See "Our Lady of the Loudspeaker," *The New Yorker* (May 25, 1928), 737-39; Joseph Henry Steele, "Sister Aimee: Bernhardt of the Sawdust Trail," *Vanity Fair* (Mar. 1933), 42; Sarah Comstock, "Aimee Semple McPherson: Prima Donna of Revivalism," *Harper's* (Dec. 1927), 11- 19; "Sister v. Satan," *Time* (Jan. 18, 1937), 32.

98. Alajalov, "Vanity Fair's Own Paper Dolls No. 2- Aimee McPherson Hutton-Caricature,"*Vanity Fair* (Nov. 1933).

99. Upton Sinclair, "An Evangelist Drowns," *New Republic* 47 (June 30, 1926), 171.

100. See Nathan Mitchell, "Aimee Semple McPherson (1890-1944): Evangelist and Innovator," *Liturgy Digest* 1:2 (1994), 44- 77, "Aimee Lives On," *Horizon* 24 (July- Aug. 1981), 18- 19; Jack Belsom, "Operatic Aimee," *Opera* 35 (Aug. 1984), 867-68; J. Kingston Pierce, "The Abduction of Aimee," *American History* 34:6 (Feb. 2000), 41-50; Frederic D Schwarz, "Aimee And Coue Improve Your Life," *American Heritage* 48 (Dec. 1997), 95-97; and Eric Lichtblau, "Faithful of 'Sister Aimee' Say Mock Court Has Redeemed Her," *Los Angeles Times* (Oct. 9, 1990), B-3.

101. Deborah George and Art Silverman, producers, Lost and Found Sound: Aimee Semple McPherson-An Oral Mystery. Full Text of NPR's "All Things Considered," November 26, 1999.

102. Blumhofer, *Everybody's Sister*, 388.

Ida Robinson

I. "Ida Robinson," in *African American Women: A Biographical Dictionary*, ed. Dorothy Salem (New York: Garland Press, 1993).

2. Rosalie Owens, "Bishop Ida Bell Robinson- 'Woman Thou Art Loosed,'" *Yes Lord, Now!* (January/February 2002), SO.

3. Mt. Sinai United Holy Church of America, Inc., *Commemorative Journal of the Mount Sinai Holy Church of America, Inc.: Serving God with What We Have.* (Philadelphia: Mt. Sinai United Holy Church of America, 1989), 139.

4. Telephone interview with Elder Minerva Bell, official historian of the Mt. Sinai Holy Church of America, October 1996.

5. Owens, "Bishop Ida Bell Robinson," 51.

6. Even though this is cited in several secondary sources, including Bell and Bell, Owens, and Larry Williams, "The Way God Led Them: A Historical Study of the Mt. Sinai Holy Church of America," DMin thesis, Howard University School of Divinity, Washington, D.C., 1998, none define what the uncomfortable situation was.

7. Mt. Sinai Holy Church of America, Inc., *Commemorative Journal*, 10.

8. Arthur H. Fauset, *Black Gods of the Metropolis: Negro Religious Cults of the Urban North* (Philadelphia: University of Pennsylvania Press, 1944), 14.

9. Mt. Sinai Holy Church of America, Inc., *Celebrating Our Legacy: History-Mt. Sinai Holy Church of America, Inc.*, vol. 1 (Philadelphia: Mt Sinai Holy Church of America, 1999), 110.

10. According to the Manual of the Mount Sinai Holy Church of America, Inc, rev. ed. (Philadelphia: Mt Sinai Holy Church of America, 1984), 11, she was noted for two songs, "What a Beautiful City" and "O I Want to See Him".

11. Felton Best, "Loosing the Women," paper presented to the Society for Pentecostal Studies, 24th Annual Meeting, Wheaton, Ill., November 1994.

12. The import of the word "publicly" is uncertain; it is unsure whether they continued ordaining women privately or what such "private" ordination would mean.

13. Cheryl Townsend Gilkes, *If It Wasn't for the Women: Black Women's Experience and Womanist Culture in Church and Community* (Maryknoll: Orbis Books, 2001), 70.

14. One of her first acts was to seek legal counsel to charter Mt. Sinai Holy Church of America, Inc. See Rosalie Owens, "Out on Mt. Sinai: How Bishop Ida Bell Robinson Loosed the Women-An Examination of her Leadership Style," Doctor of Strategic Leadership dissertation, Regent University, Center for Strategic

Leadership, March 2001, 36, or Minerva Bell, "Significant Female Leaders and Factors Leading to their Success," M.A. thesis, Farleigh Dickerson University, 1974, 50.

15. Bell and Bell, Sixty-fifth Commemorative Journal, 10.

16. Felton Best, "Loosing the Women," 9, from Mt. Sinai Holy Church of America, Inc., *Sixtieth Annual Convocation Bulletin of the Mt. Sinai Holy Church of America, Inc.*, 1984, 33.

17. Owens, "Out on Mt. Sinai," 38.

18. Ibid., 36.

19. Whether these congregations had formally joined Mt. Sinai at that time, subsequently joined, or were in fellowship with a sister organization is unknown.

20. The headquarters of the denomination has subsequently been relocated back to Philadelphia and Mt. Olive again serves as the mother church.

21. See Mt. Sinai Holy Church of America, Inc., Celebrating Our Legacy, 24-135.

22. Owens, "Out on Mt. Sinai," 30.

23. Mt. Sinai Holy Church of America, Inc., *Commemorative Journal*, 24.

24. Ibid., 25.

25. Harold Dean Trulear, "The Reshaping of Black Pastoral Theology: The Vision of Bishop Ida B. Robinson," *Journal of Religious Thought* 46 (summer-fall 1989): 24-25.

26. Ibid.

27. She apparently was no relation to Robinson but shared the same last name.

28. M. E. Wood, "What a Christian Teacher Can Do for Negro America," *Latter Day Messenger* 2:2 (1934), 4.

29. Elder Lillian Sparks, Untitled poem. *Latter Day Messenger* 2:2 (1934), 3. Adapted from a sermon by Bishop Ida Robinson.

30. Miles M. Fisher, "Organized Religion and the Cults," *Crisis* 44:1 (January 1937), 8-10.

31. Owens, "Out on Mt. Sinai," 12.

32. *Manual of the Mt. Sinai Holy Church*, 3 37.

33. Williams, "The Way God Led Them," 94.

34. See Mt. Sinai Holy Church of America, Inc., Celebrating Our Legacy, 24, and Owens, "Out on Mt. Sinai," 62.

35. Owens, "Out on Mt. Sinai," 69.

36. E. L. McCormick, "Without Honor: War on the Home Front: The Untold Story of German P.O.W.'s in Bridgeton and Fairton during World War II," South Jersey Magazine 19:1 (winter 1990), 14- 17.

37. Interview with Minerva Bell, September 23, 2001.

38. *Celebrating Our Legacy*, 140.

39. Manual of the Mt. Sinai Holy Church, 12.

40. Mt. Sinai Holy Church of America, Inc., *Commemorative Journal*, 139.

41. Fauset, Black Gods, 20.

42. Trulear, "Reshaping Black Pastoral Theology," 26-27.

43. Interview with Harold Trulear, June 20, 2001.

44. Federal Bureau of Investigation, "Foreign Inspired Agitation among the American Negroes in Philadelphia Division," File No. 100-35-37-2, Section 39497, July, 1942, and File No. 100-135-37-9, September, 1942, available under the Freedom of Information Act. Though significant information is blocked, Robinson's name is on the attached list of those under surveillance.

45. Ida Robinson, "The Economic Persecution," The Latter Day Messenger (May 23, 1935), 2. Bettye Collier-Thomas cites this work as a sermon of Robinson's in *Daughters of Thunder: Black Women and Their Sermons: 1850-1979* (San Francisco, Jossey-Bass Publishers, 1998), 203-5.

46. Robinson, "The Economic Persecution," 2.

47. Ibid.

48. Ibid.

49. Williams, "The Way God Led T hem," 89.

50.Minerva Bell, "Bishop Ida Robinson: Portrait of a Pentecostal Apostle-Founder of the Mt. Sinai Holy Church of America," paper presented to the Second Women with a Word for the Times Conference, Newport News, Virginia, April 10- 12, 1997, 5.

51. Mt. Sinai Holy Church of America, Inc., Celebrating Our Legacy, 140.

52. Estrelda Alexander, "Eva Lambert" and "Saint Mark's Holy Churches of America, Inc." in *Dictionary of Pan-African Pentecostalism, Volume 1: North America.* (Eugene, OR: Wipf & Stock, 20xx), xx

53. Trulear, "Reshaping Black Pastoral Theology"; Owens, "Out on Mt. Sinai," 61-63.

54. Owens, "Out on Mt. Sinai," 60.

55. Ibid., 50.

56. This structure was put in place possibly as early as with the initial charter, obtained by Robinson in 1924.

57. Felton Best, "Breaking the Gender Barrier," in Felton Best, *Black Religious Leadership from the Slave Community to the Million Man March: Flames of Fire*, Black Studies vol. 3 (Lewiston, NY: Edwin Mellen Press, 1998), 159.

58. As with most Pentecostal bodies, often women were sent to "preach out" new congregations. However, unlike many other bodies, Mt. Sinai women were not replaced with male pastors once congregations achieved viability.

59. Williams, "The Way God Led Them," 83.

60. Ibid.

61. Fauset, Black Gods, 14.

62. Valerie G. Lowe, "The Lady Is a Warrior" Charisma 22:8 (March 1997), 25-32.

63. The succeeding presiding bishop is elected by the board of bishops at the time of the death of the existing presiding bishop.

64. Mt. Sinai Holy Church of America, Inc., Celebrating Our Legacy, 142-43.

65. Ibid., 148.

66. Fauset, *Black Gods*, 14.

67. Mt. Sinai Holy Church of America, Inc., Celebrating Our Legacy, 148.

68. Ibid., 5-6. According to Williams, in "The Way God Led Them," 95, Stevens' husband, Charles, was nominated as president at age ninety-one but declined in her favor, due to his age.

69. Harold Dean Trulear, "Ida Robinson" in Dictionary of Pentecostal and Charismatic Movements, ed. Stanley M. Burgess, Gary R. McGee, and Patrick H. Alexander (Grand Rapids, MI: Zondervan Publishing, 1988), 762.

70. Trulear, "Reshaping Black Pastoral Theology," 30.

71. Ibid.

72. Ibid.

73. Ibid., 31.

74. Trulear hints at this connection in "The Reshaping of Black Pastoral Theology." One consequence of the lack of primary sources on Robinson is that no lengthy explication of her theological views are available.

75. Trulear, "Ida Robinson" (emphasis my own).

76. Mt. Sinai Holy Church of America, Inc., Celebrating Our Legacy, 204.

77. New congregations are planted, but older and generally more progressive congregations pull out. For example, in 2001 several congregations pulled to protest the new leadership's conservative stance on social issues and personal piety.

78. "Daughters of Thunder," 194.

79. Again, the issue is "full clergy rights." Even within Mt. Sinai, institutional positions of governance, including the bishopric, are reserved for ordained clergy.

80. Best, "Loosing the Women," 10.

81. Within Mt. Sinai, ordination and ministerial placement are not linked . An individual may be ordained a minister or elder and not serve in pastoral ministry. The person would most likely serve as an itinerant evangelist or in some other supportive position such as assistant pastor. While the pastorate is not linked to ordination, one is more likely to be assigned to a pastorate if fully ordained.

Conclusion

1. The title "bishop" is more widely used in African American than white Pentecostal bodies. The Church of God in Christ and United Holy Church use it, while the Assemblies of God and, until recently, the Church of God have not used it.

2. A repeating theme within the Pentecostal movement distinguishes between using spiritual and secular means to overcome adversity.

3. Crawford's and McPherson's organizations have remained among the most racially integrated white Pentecostal bodies.

4. For a discussion of her mental and emotional condition at the time surrounding her death, see "The Final Years," in Daniel Epstein, Sister Aimee: The Life of Amy Semple McPherson (New York: Harcourt, Brace, Jovanovich, 1993), 355-440.

Selected Bibliography

Alexander, Estrelda. *The Women of Azusa Street*. Cleveland, OH: Pilgrim Press, 2005.

Apostolic Faith Mission. *A Great Religious Leader: A Brief Sketch of the Life and Labor of Florence L. (Mother) Crawford; Founder of the Apostolic Faith Mission*. Portland OR: Apostolic Faith Publishing House, 1965.

_____. *An Historical Account of the Apostolic Faith, a Trinitarian-Fundamental Evangelistic Organization: Its Origin, Functions, Doctrinal Heritage, and Departmental Activities of Evangelism*. Portland, OR: Apostolic Faith Publishing House, 1965.

Austin, Alvyn, Aimee Semple McPherson. Don Mills, Ont.: Fitzhenry and Whiteside, 1980.

Bahr, Robert. *Least of All Saints: The Story of Aimee Semple McPherson*. Englewood Cliffs, NJ: Prentice-Hall, 1979.

Bell, Minerva. Confirming Our Earthly Heritage: Mount Sinai Heritage and Roots. Address delivered at the Sixtieth Annual Convocation of the Mt. Sinai Holy Church, September 1984 in Philadelphia, PA.

_____. "Bishop Ida Robinson: Portrait of a Pentecostal Apostle-Founder of the Mt. Sinai Holy Church of America." Paper delivered to the Second Women with a Word for the Times Conference, Newport News, VA, April 10-12, 1997.

Best, Felton. "African American Women and Leadership in the Pentecostal Church: The Mount Sinai Example." Paper delivered at the Annual Meeting of the Association for the Study of Afro-American Life and History, Dayton, OH, 1989.

_____. Black Religious Leadership from the Slave Community to the Million Man March: Flames of Fire. Black Studies volume 3. Lewiston, NY: Edwin Mellen Press, 1998.

_____. "Loosing the Women." Paper presented to the Society for Pentecostal Studies, 24th Annual Meeting, Wheaton, IL, November 1994.

Blumhofer, Edith. *Aimee Semple McPherson: Everybody's Sister*. Grand Rapids, Mich.: Wm. B. Eerdmans, 1993.

_____. "Women in Evangelicalism and Pentecostalism." In *Women and Church: The Challenge of Ecumenical Solidarity in an Age of Alienation*, ed. Melanie A. May. Grand Rapids, Mich.: William B. Eerdmans, for Commission on Faith and Order, National Council of the Churches of Christ in the USA, 1991, 3-7. (Faith and Order Series).

Chavez, Mark. *Ordaining Women: Culture and Conflict in Religious Organizations.* Cambridge, MA: Harvard University Press, 1997.

Church of the Living God, Inc. Our General Assembly, October 1977. Church of the Living God, the Pillar and Ground of the Truth, Inc. Annual General Assembly. Nashville, TN, 1988-1991.

_____. *The Constitution, Government, and General Decree Book.* Nashville: New and Living Way Publishing, 1924.

_____. *Minister's Guide and Handbook.* Nashville, TN: New and Living Way Publishing, n.d.

Church of the Living God (House of God) Pillar and Ground of the Truth Which He Purchased with His Own Blood, Inc. "Welcome to the Church of the Living God." http://www.codgnet.org.Accessed May 18, 2002

Clark, Elmer T. *The Small Sects in America.* Rev. ed. New York: Abingdon-Cokesbury Press, 1949.

Clemmons, Ithiel. *Bishop C. H. Mason and the Roots of the Church of God in Christ.* Bakersfield, CA: Pneuma Life Publishers, 1996.

Collier-Thomas, Bettye. *Daughters of Thunder: Black Women and Their Sermons,* 1850-1979. San Francisco: Jossey-Bass, 1998.

Conn, Charles W. *Where the Saints Have Trod.* Cleveland, TN: Pathway Press, 1959.

Cornwall, Robert D. "Primitivism and the Redefinition of Dispensationalism in the Theology of Aimee Semple McPherson." *Pneuma* 14 (spring 1992): 23-42.

Crawford, Florence. "Greater than Solomon." In *Sermons and Scriptural Studies.* Portland, OR: Apostolic Faith Mission, 1965, 53-54.

Crawford, Raymond. *The Light of Life Brought Healing: A Brief Sketch of the Life and Labors of Florence L. (Mother) Crawford 1872-1936.* Portland, OR.: Apostolic Faith Publishing House, 1955.

Crawford, Robert. Sermons and Scriptural Studies. Portland, OR: Apostolic Faith Publishing House, 1965.

Dayton, Lucile S., and Donald Dayton. "Women in the Holiness Movement." Paper delivered at the 106th Annual Convention of the Christian Holiness Association, Louisville, KY, April 17-19, 1974.

Deno, Vivian. "God, Authority, and the Home: Gender, Race, and U.S. Pentecostals." *Journal of Women's History* 16:3 (fall 2004): 83-105.

Dupree, Sherry, and Herbert Dupree, eds. *Exposed/!!: Federal Bureau of Investigation (FBI) Unclassified Reports on Churches and Church Leaders.* Washington, DC: Mid-Atlantic Regional Press, 1993.

Epstein, Daniel M. Sister Aimee: The Life of Amy Semple McPherson. New York: Harcourt, Brace, Jovanovich, 1993.

_____."The Legacy of Aimee Semple McPherson." *Foursquare World Advance* 36:6 (July- August 2000): 6-9.

Fauset, Arthur Huff. *Black Gods of the Metropolis: Negro Religious Cults of the Urban North*. Philadelphia PA: University of Pennsylvania Press, 1944.

Federal Bureau of Investigation. *Foreign Inspired Agitation among the American Negroes in Philadelphia Division. File No. 100-135-37-2, Section 39497*. Philadelphia, PA: Federal Bureau of Investigation, July, 1942.

_____. *Foreign Inspired Agitation among the American Negroes in Philadelphia Division. File No. 100-135-37-9*. Philadelphia, PA: Federal Bureau of Investigation. September, 1942.

Gilkes, Cheryl Townsend. *If It Wasn't for the Women: Black Women's Experience and Womanist Culture in Church and Community*. Maryknoll, NY: Orbis Books, 2001.

_____. "The Role of Women in the Sanctified Church." *Journal of Religious Thought* 43:1 (Spring- Summer 1986): 24-41.

House of God Which Is the Church of the Living God (House of God) Pillar and Ground of the Truth, without Controversy, Inc. official website. http://hogc.org.

The House of God Which is the Church of the Living God, the Pillar and Ground of the Truth, without Controversy, Inc. *The Constitution, Government, and General Decree Book*, 3rd rev. ed. Philadelphia, PA, 1936.

_____. *Official Manual of the Church of the Living God (House of God) Pillar and Ground of the Truth, without Controversy, Inc.* n.d.

Jones, Pearl W. "A Minority Report: Black Pentecostal Women." *Spirit: A Journal Incident to Black Pentecostalism* 1 (1977): 31-44.

Kershner, John J. *The Disappearance of Aimee Semple McPherson. Los Angeles*: Gem Publishing, 1926.

LaBerge, Agnes N. 0. What God Hath Wrought. New York: Garland Press, 1985. Originally published by Herald Publishing, Chicago, IL, 1920.

Lewis, Helen M., and Meharry H. Lewis. *The Beauty of Holiness: A Small Catechism of the Holiness Faith and Doctrine*. Nashville: New and Living Way Publishing, 1988.

_____. *Seventy-Fifth Anniversary Yearbook of the Church of the Living God, the Pillar and Ground of the Truth, Inc. 1903-1978*. Nashville: New and Living Way Publishing, 1978.

Lewis, Meharry H. *Mary Lena Lewis Tate - A Street Called Straight: The Ten Most Dynamic and Productive Black Female Holiness Preachers of the Twentieth Century*, Nashville, TN: New & Living Way Publishing, 1989.

_____."Mary Lena Tate: VISION!" *In Founders Day Recognition: Our 89th Year by Church of the Living God, the Pillar and Ground of the Truth*, January 25, 1992), 4.

Mavity, Nancy Barr. Sister Aimee. Garden City, NY: Doubleday, Doran & Company, 1931.

McLaughlin, William G. "Aimee Semple McPherson: Your Sister in the King's Glad Service." In *Modern American Protestantism and Its World*, ed. Marty E. Martin. Vol. 3, Women and Women's Issues, 119-44. Munich: K.G. Saur, 1993.

McPherson, Aimee Semple. *The Foursquare Gospel*. Los Angeles: Echo Park Evangelistic Association, 1946.

_____. *The Story of My Life*. Waco, TX: Word Publications, 1973. Originally published, Los Angeles: Echo Park Evangelistic Association, 1927.

_____. *This Is That*. Los Angeles, New York: Garland Publications, 1985. Originally published, Los Angeles: Echo Park Evangelistic Association, 1919.

Mendiola, Kelly. "The Hand of Woman: Four Holiness-Pentecostal Evangelists and American Culture, 1840-1930." PhD dissertation, University of Texas at Austin, 2002.

Mt. Sinai Holy Church of America, Inc. *Commemorative Journal of the Mount Sinai Holy Church of America, Inc.: Serving God with What We Have*. Philadelphia: Mt Sinai Holy Church of America, 1989.

_____. *Celebrating Our Legacy: History - Mt. Sinai Holy Church of America, Inc., Volume 1*. Philadelphia: Mt Sinai Holy Church of America, 1999.

_____. *Manual of the Mount Sinai Holy Church of America, Inc.* Rev. ed. Philadelphia: Mt Sinai Holy Church of America, 1984.

Owens, Rosalie. *Out on Mt. Sinai: How Bishop Ida Bell Robinson Loosed the Women-An Examination of Her Leadership Style*. Doctor of Strategic Leadership dissertation, Regent University, Center for Strategic Leadership, March 2001.

Pierce, J. Kingston. "The Abduction of Aimee." *American History* 34:6 (fall, 2000.

Poloma, Margaret. *The Assemblies of God at the Crossroads*. Knoxville: University of Tennessee Press, 1989.

Robeck, Cecil M., Jr. "Florence Crawford: Apostolic Faith Pioneer." In *Portraits of a Generation: Early Pentecostal Leaders* by Grant Wacker and James Goff, Fayetteville: University of Arkansas Press, 2002, 219-35.

Scanzoni, Letha, and Susan Setta. "Women in Evangelical, Holiness, and Pentecostal Traditions." In *Women and Religion in America*. Vol. 3, 1900-1968, ed. Rosemary Radford Ruether and Rosemary Skinner Keller, Cambridge, MA: Harper and Row Publishers, 1986, 223- 35.

Shuford, F. Dovie. "Mother Mary Magdalena L. Tate (1871-1930)." In *Profiles of African Americans in Tennessee*, ed. Bobby L. Lovett and Linda T. Wynn. Nashville, Tenn.: Annual Local Conference on Afro-American Culture and History, 1996.

217

Shuler, Robert Pierce. *"McPhersonism": A Study of Healing Cults and the Modern Day "Tongues" Movements.* Los Angeles: n.p., n.d.

Thomas, Lately. *Storming Heaven: the Lives and Turmoils of Minnie Kennedy and Aimee Semple McPherson.* New York: Morrow, 1970.

Townsend, Gregg D. "The Material Dream of Aimee Semple McPherson: A Lesson in Pentecostal Spirituality." *Pneuma* 1 4 (Spring 1992): 23-42.

Trulear, Harold Dean. "The Reshaping of Black Pastoral Theology: The Vision of Bishop Ida B. Robinson." *Journal of Religious Thought* 46 (Summer-Fall, 1989): 17-31.

_____. "There's a Bright Side Somewhere." *Journal of African American Historical and Genealogical Society* 2 (1987): 51-56.

United Holy Church of America. *Standard Manual and Constitution and By-Laws of the United Holy Church of America, Incorporated.* Washington, D.C.: Middle Atlantic Regional Press, 1988.

_____. *Standard Manual of the United Holy Church of America and Constitution and By-Laws.* Greensboro, NC: Church, 1997.

Index

CPSIA information can be obtained
at www.ICGtesting.com
Printed in the USA
LVHW081518050822
725284LV00015B/1368

9 781938 373497